SEVEN TRAITS

OF A SUCCESSFUL LEADER

A PILGRIMAGE
SMALL GROUP GUIDE BY
JEFFREY ARNOLD

NAVPRESS

BRINGING TRUTH TO LIFE
NavPress Publishing Group
P.O. Box 35001, Colorado Springs, Colorado 80935

The Navigators is an international Christian organization. Our mission is to reach, disciple, and equip people to know Christ and to make Him known through successive generations. We envision multitudes of diverse people in the United States and every other nation who have a passionate love for Christ, live a lifestyle of sharing Christ's love, and multiply spiritual laborers among those without Christ.

NavPress is the publishing ministry of The Navigators. NavPress publications help believers learn biblical truth and apply what they learn to their lives and ministries. Our mission is to stimulate spiritual formation among our readers.

Cover photo: PhotoDisc

Pilgrimage small group study guides are published in conjunction with The Pilgrimage Group, an organization that trains pastors and lay leaders across the United States and Canada in the essentials of small group ministry and leadership. For more information on Pilgrimage training or consulting, call 1-800-477-7787. Or, visit the Pilgrimage web site at http//www.pilgrimage.org/training/.

Unless otherwise identified, all Scripture quotations in this publication are taken from the *HOLY BIBLE: NEW INTERNATIONAL VERSION* ® (NIV®). Copyright © 1973, 1978, 1984 by International Bible Society, used by permission of Zondervan Publishing House, all rights reserved. The other version used is *The Message* (MSG) by Eugene H. Peterson, copyright © 1993, 1994, 1995, 1996, used by permission of NavPress Publishing Group.

Printed in the United States of America

1 2 3 4 5 6 7 8 9 10 11 12 13 14 15 / 02 01 00 99 98 97

Contents

How This Study Guide Works

Training Leaders

There is a leadership crisis in the church and world today.

Our political leaders seem unwilling to make difficult choices. Our cultural and sports leaders tend to live in a self-absorbed manner. Our community leaders are required to allocate limited resources to meet seemingly unlimited needs. Our religious leaders discover that their training is inadequate for the fast-changing and complex times in which we live.

Unfortunately, nobody benefits from a leaderless world. Our societal problems require deep questions and spiritual answers. Solutions will not be found as long as today's problems are being answered by yesterday's solutions.

We need a new wave of leaders. Commissioned by Jesus, these leaders will cloak themselves in God-centered traits, having been set apart for the kingdom-building that must be done. The contrast between worldly leadership and godly leadership is, as Jesus' life demonstrates, eye-catching and contagious.

Missionary John Paton is an example of such leadership. In the early 1800s, Paton and his family landed on the New Hebrides Islands in the South Pacific to evangelize among cannibals. By the time he left the islands years later, the island residents had been thoroughly touched by the gospel. In the meantime, Paton had lost his wife and child to disease; his life had been threatened countless times; and he had fought loneliness and disease in a one-man battle to share the gospel with a resistant clientele.

Paton performed his work without the latest in demographic data. He did not have sociological studies on the mindsets of cannibals. He was not highly trained in today's facilitation leadership techniques. His own autobiography details his struggles with loneliness, frustration, fear, and the threat of being sacrificed and eaten.

Yet Paton succeeded in his endeavor. He led countless cannibals to Christ and helped to establish a Christ-centered beachhead in a godless land. How did he succeed? He clung tenaciously to his faith and he was a person in whom God's leadership traits were evident.

The goal of this resource is to equip a new generation of courageous leaders who, like John Paton, demonstrate healthy traits in their lifestyle and interactions. Leadership support groups using this resource may include the following:

- ► small group leaders
- ► pastor support groups
- ► church leaders (elders, deacons, trustees, administrative boards)
- ► Sunday school teachers
- ► youth ministry leaders
- ► college ministry leaders
- ► children's ministry leaders
- ► committees
- ► ministry teams
- ► short-term mission groups
- ► apprentices

This resource offers growing leaders an opportunity to partner together in an exciting, relational, hands-on learning approach. Using a small group format, members will:

- ► encourage one another to learn about and exhibit traits of healthy leadership
- ► engage in individual and group reflection
- ► receive individual analysis of their traits
- ► participate in creative Bible study and group process
- ► work together to solve intriguing leadership problems
- ► learn to receive care from other leaders
- ► create a structured small group for continued leadership support and prayer
- ► practice the daily disciplines necessary to develop positive leadership traits

Why "Traits"?

Many leadership resources address both the function and vision of leadership. Their focus is on "doing." Not as many resources focus on "being." Yet Scripture makes it clear that anything good that we accomplish is more a measure of God's grace than our action (Galatians 5:22-23). In fact, Scripture assumes that even our "good" actions are nothing apart from God (Romans 3).

Resources like this one that focus on being and zero in on the marks of God's grace in our lives are indispensable. They help us to identify God's good work in our lives, so that we can offer thanks and praise. They draw us to pray for an ever deeper measure of God's grace, that we might be drawn continuously to deeper spiritual maturity. They compel us to share God's love with a frightened and hurting world. They challenge us to partner with God in ushering in His kingdom.

Why These Traits?

When preparing to write this resource, I culled leadership books (some of them appear in the resource lists following each session) and made extensive lists. I removed traits that were either redundant or otherwise closely associated with others on the list. I then grouped the remaining traits together into seven categories (see Table of Contents on page 3 for listing). Those traits that were not primary I integrated thematically into the structure of other sessions when applicable.

A process like this helps to unite themes discovered in the narrative and didactic accounts of Scripture. The purpose of this resource is to allow leaders to prayerfully study leadership traits in an interactive group environment.

The thread running through all seven traits is servanthood. We hear the term "servant leadership" often; what does it actually involve? While I deal with servant leadership most directly in session four, I believe the seven traits taken together portray what Jesus meant when he told his followers to lead as servants.

Building Community

The life of following Christ was never meant to be solitary. The early Christians pursued it in groups not much larger than your small group. They met exclusively in homes for the first two hundred years or so of the movement. By meeting in a small group, you are imitating a time-tested format for spiritual life.

People join small groups for all sorts of reasons: to get to know a few people well, to be cared for, to learn, to grow spiritually. We believe small groups are the ideal setting in which people can both learn what it means to take on the character of Christ and also practice the process of becoming like Christ. While there are many spiritually helpful things one can do alone or in a large group, a small group offers many advantages. Among other things, group members can:

- ▶ encourage one another in good times and bad
- ▶ ask thoughtful questions when a member has a decision to make
- ▶ listen to God together
- ▶ pray for each other
- ▶ benefit from one another's insights into Scripture
- ▶ acquire a habit of reading the Bible on a regular basis
- ▶ practice loving their neighbors
- ▶ worship God together
- ▶ learn to communicate effectively
- ▶ solve problems together
- ▶ learn to receive care from others
- ▶ experience the pleasure of helping another person grow

This guide emphasizes skill development and relationship-building. It will help you explore what it means to be an effective leader among the people of God. You will engage in reflection, study, interaction, problem solving, and prayer. You will be challenged to adapt personal homework electives so that you can continue exercising leadership traits during the week. You will identify who you are as a leader and what you need to work on.

A Modular Approach

Each session is divided into several modules or sections. Suggested times are allocated among the modules so that you can complete the session in 60 to 90 minutes. The modules are:

Overview: The first page of each session briefly describes the objectives for your meeting so that you will know what to expect during the meeting and what results to strive for. You will also learn something about the author's own story as it relates to the topic at hand.

Beginning: Building relationships is a necessary part of a group experience. Each session of this guide will include questions to help you learn who the other members are and where they have been in their lives. The beginning questions also help you begin thinking about a particular leadership issue in preparation for a time of Bible study and problem solving.

The Text: Studying a biblical text is an integral part of this guide. You will examine brief passages from various parts of the Bible. THE MESSAGE by Eugene Peterson and THE NEW INTERNATIONAL VERSION have been chosen where appropriate. THE MESSAGE is deliberately relational and will help those familiar with Scripture to see certain passages with new eyes. Since the New Testament was written to be read aloud, you will begin your study by reading the text aloud. Words in bold type are explained in the Reference Notes section.

Understanding the Text: Unless you notice carefully what the text says, you will not be able to interpret it accurately. The questions in this section will help you focus on the key issues and wrestle with what the text means.

Applying the Text: It is not enough to simply understand the passage; you need to apply that understanding to your situation. The questions in this section connect what you have read to how you live. This section will encourage you to do problem solving and creative application of leadership traits.

Assignment: To allow for flexibility with both groups and individuals, this guide offers homework electives. The Bible study elective suggests scriptures to read and reflect on. The reflection elective encourages you to identify where you are as a leader and what you need to work on. The project elective gives you simple tasks to perform. At the end of each session, your group can choose which, if any, of these electives to pursue before your next meeting. You may decide that everyone will do the same homework; this choice will enable you to compare notes and support each other in the same discipline. On the other hand, you may prefer to let each person choose the homework style that best suits him or her.

Prayer: Praying together can be one of the most faith-building and relationship-building things you do together. Suggestions are made to facilitate this time in the group.

Reference Notes: In order to understand the meaning of the text, one needs to know a little about the context in which it was written and the key words and phrases it contains. The notes include background on the characters, information about cultural practices, word definitions, and so on. You will find entries in this section for those words and phrases in the text that are printed in bold type. You can scan the notes after reading the text aloud, or during your discussion of Understanding the Text.

Additional Resources: A few suggestions for further reading will be offered in relation to the chapter's topic.

Help for the Leader

This guide provides everything the leader needs to facilitate the group's discussion. In each session, the ❶ symbol designates instructions for the leader. Since this group is for leaders, you may consider alternating each week.

Answers to Common Questions

Who is this material designed for?
- ▶ Any persons who want to challenge themselves to more effective leadership.
- ▶ Leaders who want the support that a small group offers.

How often should we meet?
- ▶ Once a week is best; every other week works as well; and some churches will encourage their leaders to use this resource once per month.

How long should we meet?
- ▶ You will need at least an hour.
- ▶ Ninety minutes is best—this gives time for more discussion.
- ▶ Some groups may want to meet for two hours, especially if you have more than eight people.

What if we have only 50 minutes?
- ▶ Cut back on the Beginning section and adapt the Applying the Text problem solvers. Read the text quickly and pray only briefly.

Is homework necessary?
- ▶ No, the group can meet with no prior preparation.
- ▶ The assignments, especially the project and reflection, will greatly increase what you gain from the group.

Significant Relationships

Overview ▼ ▼ ▼ ▼ ▼ ▼ ▼ ▼ ▼ ▼ ▼ ▼ ▼ ▼ ▼ ▼ ▼ ▼ 10 minutes

❶ *Welcome: Make sure that everybody has been welcomed to the group and that the room is comfortably arranged. If leaders do not know each other, exchange names. If they do not know you, introduce yourself to the group, sharing:*

- ▶ *your name*
- ▶ *your leadership role*
- ▶ *several objectives you have for this leadership group*

If there are others sharing leadership responsibility with you, perhaps a host/hostess, introduce them as well. Then, briefly sketch out your agenda for the meeting. What should people expect to happen? Pass out discussion guides if necessary. Then ask someone to read aloud this story and the objectives that follow.

I was invited to speak at a retreat a number of years ago. My girlfriend, Karen (now my wife), was asked to attend as well.

As the bus pulled out of the church and headed for the mountains, I told Karen, "I'll see you at the end of the retreat. It is time for me to do ministry." For the next three days I worked with passion, motivated both by the winning of souls and the impressing of my future wife.

At the end of the retreat, I located Karen. "So, how did I

11

do?" I still cringe at her response. "You are the sorriest excuse for a Christian leader I have ever seen!"

She was right. When she met me I was a seven-day-a-week workaholic with no deep relationships. How could I call people to a deep experience with God that I was not having? How could I teach them about the community of faith if I dwelt on the periphery?

I realize now that I was running from community for fear of being hurt. Persons in all levels of ministry learn that people can hurt. We begin to protect ourselves beneath layers of work, shallow relationships, deep studies, and decisions that must be made.

God has been dealing with my workaholic motives, most notably my fear of intimacy. He provided a spouse and children, who break into my world and include me in theirs. I have begun to nurture deep friendships, opening myself to more risk and also more blessing.

The foundation of effective leadership is the ability to sustain lasting, growing relationships. If we can't sustain deep, real relationships, we can't grow in such fruits of the Spirit as love, kindness, and gentleness. In this session we will:

▶ discuss the various relationships leaders are involved in and through which they can model a Christian lifestyle

▶ examine what Scripture has to say about a leader's relationships

▶ prepare to examine our own lives in light of what we learn

▼ ▼ ▼ ▼ ▼ ▼ ▼ ▼ ▼ ▼ ▼ ▼ ▼ ▼ ▼ ▼ ▼ ▼

Beginning   15 minutes

❶ *Read aloud this explanation of sharing questions.*

Everybody has been affected by role models and leaders, both positively and negatively. By sharing our stories with each other, we will learn about one another and begin to discover how we can affect each others' lives for good. We will earn each other's trust by giving and receiving our stories.

Go around the room and allow each person to answer the first question before moving to the next one. The leader should answer first each time.

1. When you were a child (ages 7-12), which of the following best characterized you?

☐ a participant—part of the group
☐ a loner—off by myself
☐ a leader—got people organized
☐ a friend—with a small circle of intimate peers
☐ an individualist—could operate alone or in crowds
☐ other:

2. As you look back over your life, who is a person or leader who influenced you in a positive way?

3. As you look back over your life, who is a person or leader who influenced you in a negative way?

▼ ▼
The Text   5 minutes

First Timothy is often called a "pastoral epistle" because in it the apostle Paul mentors his young apprentice, Timothy, in issues related to Christian leadership. Timothy was already a pastor and facing problems among the collection of home-based churches he led. From 1 and 2 Timothy we can discern that Timothy's community was experiencing division, gossip, disruptions in worship, challenges to Timothy's leadership, poor administration, and other problems.

In the passage we are about to study, Paul identifies the kind of leaders the people of God need in order to grow.

❶ *Have someone read the text aloud. You may also read some or all of the reference notes on pages 20-21.*

If anyone wants to provide **leadership** in the church, good! But there are preconditions: A leader must be well-thought-of, **committed to his wife,** cool and collected, accessible, and hospitable. He must know what he's talking about, not be overfond of wine,

13

not pushy but gentle, not thin-skinned, not money-hungry. He must handle his own affairs well, attentive to his own children and having their respect. For if someone is unable to handle his own affairs, how can he take care of God's church? He must not be a **new believer,** lest the position go to his head and the Devil trip him up. Outsiders must think well of him, or else **the Devil will figure out a way to lure him into his trap.**

The same goes for those who want to be servants in the church: serious, not deceitful, not too free with the bottle, not in it for what they can get out of it. They must be reverent before the mystery of the faith, not using their position to try to run things. Let them prove themselves first. If they show they can do it, take them on. **No exceptions are to be made for women**—same qualifications: serious, dependable, not sharp-tongued, not overfond of wine. Servants in the church are to be committed to their spouses, attentive to their own children, and diligent in looking after their own affairs. Those who do this servant work will come to be highly respected, a real credit to this Jesus-faith.

(1 Timothy 3:1-13, MSG)

▼ ▼ ▼ ▼ ▼ ▼ ▼ ▼ ▼ ▼ ▼ ▼ ▼ ▼ ▼ ▼ ▼ ▼
Understanding the Text   20 minutes

4. This passage mentions at least six different kinds of relation-ships in which leaders operate. Using specific references from the passage, describe how a leader should be relating to:

    ❏ God
    ❏ God's people
    ❏ those who don't know Christ, including work associates and neighbors
    ❏ family

5. Why do you suppose Paul stresses the qualities of a person's relationships when he lists qualifications for leadership?

Mike is an elder in the Jerusalem Community Church. He is a hard-working man, well thought of in church and community. He has brought many of his friends into the church, and shares preaching and teaching responsibilities with several other elders. Nobody would have a concern about Mike, except for one thing: his wife is unhappy with her marriage. She talks in the church about how distant, irritable, and controlling Mike can be at home. She notes that their children feel their father has no time or energy for them—and that the children are starting to rebel. She accuses him of being a workaholic. Some in the church are beginning to realize that Mike can be "hot and cold" in the way that he interacts with people. Sometimes he appears caring, and other times distant.

6. a. Based on this scenario and the passage in 1 Timothy, how would you respond to Mike's wife?

   b. What counsel would you give Mike?

   c. What, if anything, should the church do in relation to Mike?

▼▼▼▼▼▼▼▼▼▼▼▼▼▼▼▼▼▼
Applying the Text   20 minutes

It is difficult to know how to deal with people like Mike (and you and me). On the one hand are statements in Scripture, like this one in 1 Timothy, that list character and relational traits of leaders. Against such standards all leaders are judged. On the other hand, no one but Christ can measure up to all of the biblical lists. If we examine each leader based on absolute adherence to the biblical lists, everybody will fail and we will have no leaders. But if we do not have standards, our leadership quality diminishes and we again have no leaders. Is there a healthy middle ground?

The middle ground is that leaders must continually be nourished in their growth. Healthy leaders exhibit spiritual, emotional, mental, and relational growth. Leaders should be encouraged not to hide their weaknesses (a temptation when standards are high and "failures" are not tolerated) but to share those weaknesses with others who can help them grow.

7. Go around the room, allowing each person to answer this question: Of the following relationships, which do I feel comfortable with, and which do I need to work on?

   ❐ God
   ❐ family
   ❐ my church or faith community
   ❐ those outside my church or faith community
   ❐ work associates

8. Of the relational areas that need work, which would you like prayer for, and how can the group pray for you?

9. Read the sections TRAINING LEADERS and BUILDING COMMUNITY on pages 5-8.

   a. What aspects of these sections are most attractive to you?

   b. Does anything in these sections confuse or trouble you? Explain.

10. Discuss the following ground rules for being in this leader's group. Add to the list or adapt the list according to your situation, and then make a covenant of trust with one another. We promise to practice:

- ❏ Acceptance—To affirm one another's contributions
- ❏ Confidentiality—That what is spoken in this group will remain in the group
- ❏ Openness—That as we are able, we will be honest and forthright with one another
- ❏ Graciousness—Not to speak about a person when he or she is not present
- ❏ Self-discipline—That if the group agrees to do homework, we will come prepared
- ❏ Courtesy—That when the group meets, we will come on time
- ❏ Listening—That we will not monopolize time so that others can speak
- ❏ Other:

▼▼▼▼▼▼▼▼▼▼▼▼▼▼▼▼▼▼▼
Assignment   10 minutes

- ▶ Before you dismiss, pass around your book and have everyone sign the group phone list on page 95.

- ▶ (Optional) Ask if someone would volunteer to bring a simple snack for the next meeting.

- ▶ Decide which of the following homework electives you will do. You may choose to do the same elective or different ones. Make sure that your choices are reasonable and will be performed by everyone prior to the next meeting.

Elective 1: Bible Study—There are six Bible passages on the next page. As you read the passages, consider what they teach about the marks of God-honoring relationships.

- Day 1—Deuteronomy 6:1-9
- Day 2—Psalm 23
- Day 3—Proverbs 3:1-12
- Day 4—John 17
- Day 5—1 Corinthians 13
- Day 6—1 John 4:7-21

Elective 2: Reflection—Begin a journal, which you will keep during the next seven weeks and hopefully continue after the course is done. Purchase a notebook and put your name on the outside. For this week's reflection, put a heading like "Healthy Relationships" at the top of the first page. Then devote at least one page to exploring each of the following relationships: God; family (if you have no immediate family, then think about extended family); church or faith community; work/neighborhood; those who don't know Christ. To guide your exploration, consider the following suggestions:

- Make the reflection in the form of a letter to the person(s) if that helps you to be more creative.
- Consider how your relationship is positive and blesses your life.
- Consider the ways that your relationship needs work to become more a model of God's love.
- Consider past hurts (both by you and to you) that have never been addressed.

Elective 3: Project—Bring the following list of complaints to a friend or family member who knows you well and who can be honest with you. As you read the complaint and he or she responds, make a mark in the appropriate column. Don't ask the person to defend his or her answer; just receive it (you can discuss it after you've had time to reflect). When you're finished, go back over the list on your own to see potential areas of growth.

Complaint:

	Often	Seldom	Never
1. Doesn't allow me to explain what my problems are.	❑	❑	❑
2. Never lets me complete more than a few sentences before interrupting. Acts as if it is hard to wait until I finish.	❑	❑	❑

	Often	*Seldom*	*Never*

3. Is distant and doesn't pay attention when I speak.

   ☐   ☐   ☑

4. Is too busy doing his or her own thing to take an interest in mine or another's.

   ☐   ☑   ☐

5. Has a way of putting me on the defensive or confusing me when I am trying to make a point.

   ☐   ☑   ☐

6. Is irritable much of the time, making me and others feel like we make his or her life miserable.

   ☐   ☐   ☑

7. Complains much of the time.

   ☐   ☐   ☑

8. Does not model a compassionate, patient, loving person to family or friends.

   ☐   ☑   ☐

▼▼▼▼▼▼▼▼▼▼▼▼▼▼▼▼▼▼
Prayer   5 minutes

Stand in a circle. Allow each person to answer this question:

"As we close this session, I feel. . . ."

- ☐ convicted
- ☐ fearful
- ☐ hopeful
- ☐ excited
- ☐ other

Hold hands if you are comfortable doing so. Let each person pray aloud, beginning with the leader. Consider praying by name for the leaders in your group, listing the requests that they made under Applying the Text. If you would rather pray silently, please say "Amen" aloud to let the other people know you are finished.

▼ ▼
Reference Notes

Setting: Timothy was a young pastor whom Paul had left behind in Ephesus. Paul had not been able to return, and he had heard of problems his young protégé was encountering. There was false teaching, strife and division, a false sense of piety, laziness, and gossip. In this context it was appropriate that Paul identified leadership traits expected of both Timothy and those who were serving the church at Ephesus. Chances are that although Paul wrote this letter to Timothy personally, he intended the whole community of Ephesian believers to hear and understand what Paul expected from their leaders.

leadership: The Greek word is *episcopae.* This word literally means "overseer." In the second century AD it became the formal office of "bishop." Other New Testament passages speak of elders and deacons, suggesting that the New Testament church offered some variation in positions of leadership. An "overseer" is one who leads—by administering, guiding, and modeling. The context ("If anyone sets his heart on being an overseer, he desires a noble task") suggests that in the early church the formal positions of leadership were either abused or looked down upon.

committed to his wife: Throughout history this passage has been used to prohibit among church leaders such practices as polygamy, remarriage after divorce, or a second marriage after the death of a spouse. It has also been used to require all bishops to be married. How should we understand this passage today? I think Eugene Peterson's translation of the passage is close to the spirit of the text: A leader must be committed to his or her spouse. A healthy family models intimacy to a disconnected world. The ideal is for a person to be married (if at all) once, and out of the strength of that marriage to serve God. Those who are unable, for various reasons, to develop lasting relationships (especially those who claim to be Christian and who have been divorced more than once) should willingly step back from leadership and grow stronger in faith and practice.

new believer: The word "recent convert" is *neophutos,* from which we derive our word "neophyte." It literally means "newly planted," a visual image suggesting a vulnerable, tender plant not yet tested by the elements. True to all images of childhood, pride is an especially strong temptation for new believers. The church in Ephesus was loaded with new believers who were pressing Timothy for representation and leadership. Paul encouraged the believers to wait, to allow the process of spiritual growth to catch up with them, and to test their lives against the traits listed in this passage.

the Devil will figure out a way to lure him into his trap: The question is, what trap? And what is the result of a new convert being lured into Satan's trap? The answer is most likely located in the context: "Outsiders must think well of him." Why would outsiders not think well of a new convert and aspiring leader? And what happens if outsiders do not think well of an aspiring leader? First, an aspiring leader who is young in the faith is prone to excesses that are tempered with spiritual growth. A new convert can be controlling, demanding, and judgmental. When outsiders begin to withdraw, he or she will tend to judge those persons pridefully and may isolate from others. Satan's trap is to remove us from the community of faith and destroy us—and young leaders are especially susceptible.

No exceptions are to be made for women: Space does not permit us to thoroughly address the issue of women in ministry. This passage is obviously written primarily addressing men's circumstances— until verse 11. At that point women are introduced, but in a manner that is subject to extensive debate. Does verse 11 imply women in all aspects in ministry, as Peterson's translation suggests? Or does it apply either to elders' or deacons' wives? Or only to deacons' wives? Or to deaconesses? Without changing the meaning of the text we can discern general principles for women who serve in ministry. They are to be "serious, dependable, not sharp-tongued, not overfond of wine . . . committed to their spouses, attentive to their own children, and diligent in looking after their own affairs."

▼ ▼ ▼ ▼ ▼ ▼ ▼ ▼ ▼ ▼ ▼ ▼ ▼ ▼ ▼ ▼ ▼ ▼ ▼ ▼
Additional Resources

1. Arnold, Jeffrey. *The Big Book on Small Groups.* Downers Grove, Ill.: InterVarsity, 1991.

2. Hauerwas, Stanley and Will Willimon. *Resident Aliens.* Nashville, Tenn.: Abingdon, 1989.

3. Pinnock, Clark and Robert Brow. *Unbounded Love: A Good News Theology for the 21st Century.* Downers Grove, Ill.: InterVarsity, 1994.

4. Stedman, Ray. *Body Life.* Ventura, Calif.: Regal, 1972.

▼ ▼ ▼ ▼ ▼ ▼ ▼ ▼ ▼ ▼ ▼ ▼ ▼ ▼ ▼ ▼ ▼ ▼
Food for Thought

"The first responsibility of a leader is to define reality. The last is to say thank you. In between the two, the leader must become *a servant and a debtor*. That sums up the progress of an artful leader."

Max DuPres,
Leadership is An Art,
(New York: Doubleday, 1989),
p. 9 (emphasis added).

Faith

▼▼ ▼ ▼ ▼ ▼ ▼ ▼ ▼ ▼ ▼ ▼ ▼ ▼ ▼ ▼ ▼
Overview   10 minutes

❶ *Welcome: Make sure that any newcomers are intro-duced and given the appropriate materials. Exchange names if group members' memories need to be refreshed.*

Allow several group members to share what they learned from their homework (if the group did not do homework, encourage members to recap what they learned from the last session). Then ask someone to read aloud this story and the objectives that follow.

Eager to build significant relationships with the members of the group he was leading, Phil met Dave for lunch at a local diner. During the course of their conversation, Phil asked what he thought was a non-threatening question: "How do you feel our group is going?"

Dave's facial expression changed. "I don't know if we should talk about this now."

Phil leaned back in the booth (a subconscious gesture con-ditioned by having participated in similar conversations before). "You can be honest with me."

"But I don't want to hurt you."

Phil crossed his arms (another subconscious gesture). "No really, what is going on with you? I want to know."

"Well, some of the members and I have been talking. . . ."

Phil rubbed his face with his hands and pressed his eyelids closed with his thumb and forefinger.

". . . and we don't like the direction the group is going. We're just not getting anywhere. . . ."

Anybody involved in ministry for long knows that situations like this present themselves at irregular intervals. They usually occur when a leader is already feeling vulnerable. The resulting anguish can feel like a kick in the gut.

Leaders confront many varied, complicated situations. They discover that they are inextricably linked to what is going on around them. Leadership might feel more palatable if we were able to sit outside all situations and manage them. However, our proximity to the action means that we will sometimes get wounded in the line of fire.

God allows it to be that way. Christian love is expressed through such unlikely means as risk, personal pain, and willingness to pay a price for the salvation and benefit of others. Jesus Christ is the greatest example in history of such "incarnational" leadership.

Being an effective leader requires faith. Faith calls us to risk our very selves. In this session we will:

► discuss the principles and stages of faith development
► examine what Scripture has to say about a leader's faith
► challenge each other to the healthy risks demanded by faith
► begin to examine our lives in relation to the faith necessary to become great leaders

▼ ▼ ▼ ▼ ▼ ▼ ▼ ▼ ▼ ▼ ▼ ▼ ▼ ▼ ▼ ▼ ▼ ▼
Beginning   15 minutes

❶ *Go around the room and allow each person to answer the first question before moving to the next one. The leader should answer first each time.*

1. Pick one of the following "I have never" statements and explain why it pertains to you. I have never . . .

   ❒ confronted a person who hurt me
   ❒ invested in the stock market
   ❒ gone up to a famous person and introduced myself

☐ asked a friend's forgiveness because I had gossiped about him or her

☐ done a risky sport like bungee jumping, para-sailing, downhill skiing

☐ spoken in front of a large crowd

2. What is something risky (anything that made you nervous or fearful) you have done in your life?

3. What made you take the risk?

Worship ▼▼▼▼▼▼▼▼▼▼▼▼▼▼▼▼▼▼▼▼ 10 minutes—Optional

This is a great time to worship as a group if it fits your plan for the group and the ministry style of your church. See the worship section in the appendix. Specific worship suggestions will be provided in several later sessions.

The Text ▼▼▼▼▼▼▼▼▼▼▼▼▼▼▼▼▼▼▼▼ 5 minutes

Hebrews 11 is called the "Roll Call of Faith." It contains one of the most comprehensive statements made in Scripture about faith and lists biblical heroes who lived out their faith in powerful ways.

❶ *Have someone read the text aloud. You may also read some or all of the reference notes on page 32.*

Now faith is being sure of what we hope for and certain of what we do not see. This is what the ancients were commended for. By faith we understand that the universe was formed at God's command, so that what is seen was not made out of what was visible.

By faith Abraham, when called to go to a place he would later receive as his inheritance, obeyed and went, even though he did not know where he was going. By faith he made his home in the promised land like a stranger in a foreign country; he lived in tents, as did Isaac and Jacob, who were heirs with him of the same promise. For he was looking forward to the city with foundations, whose architect and builder is God.

By faith Abraham, even though he was past age—and Sarah herself was barren—was enabled to become a father because he considered him faithful who had made the promise. And so from this one man, and he as good as dead, came descendants as numerous as the stars in the sky and as countless as the sand on the seashore.

All these people were still living by faith when they died. They did not receive the things promised; they only saw them and welcomed them from a distance. And they admitted that they were aliens and strangers on earth. People who say such things show that they are looking for a country of their own. If they had been thinking of the country they had left, they would have had opportunity to return. Instead, they were longing for a better country—a heavenly one. Therefore God is not ashamed to be called their God, for he has prepared a city for them.

(Hebrews 11:1-3, 8-16)

▼▼▼▼▼▼▼▼ ▼ ▼ ▼ ▼ ▼ ▼ ▼ ▼▼▼
Understanding the Text   15 minutes

4. From this text and using your own words, what is faith?

FAITH IS MANY THINGS. SIMPLY IT IS BELIEVING THAT GOD IS IN CONTROL AND IN ALL CIRCUMSTANCE HE HAS A PURPOSE - SO GOOD OR BAD HIS PLAN IS SOVEREIGN AND WAS SET BEFORE THE FOUNDATIONS OF THE WORLD

5. a. Find at least three things that Abraham's faith compelled him to do.

1) TRUST – LEAVING THE THINGS BEHIND

2) BELIEVE – MOVING AHEAD TO THINGS PROMISED

3) RECEIVE – GAINING GODS BLESSING AND PERSPECTIVE

b. Since this passage says he never received what was promised, what do you think were the benefits of his living by faith?

A LEGACY – HE MAY NOT HAVE RECEIVED

TANGIBLY THE PROMISE. BUT HIS ETERNAL REWARD

WAS GAINED – HIS EYES WERE BEYOND THE HERE

AND NOW – BUT ON THIS RELATIONSHIP W THE FATHER

6. Faith does not come naturally. It grows throughout our lives as we learn to risk and trust. Our text suggests that this growth progresses through certain stages:

▶ Stage 1—Becoming aware of God (vv. 1-3).
▶ Stage 2—Leaving our past behind and becoming followers of God (vv. 8-9).
▶ Stage 3—Living a new life with new rules (vv. 10-12).
▶ Stage 4—Identifying so much with God's plans that we die to our own (vv. 13-16).

For each of these stages answer two questions.

❏ What is a person experiencing in this stage?
❏ What issues must a person deal with in this stage?

a. Stage 1

b. Stage 2

c. Stage 3

d. Stage 4

7. The last paragraph of the passage says that "All these people (Abraham and other heroes of the faith) were still living by faith when they died." It then goes on to describe several of their characteristics. In your own words, what set those people apart?

1) ETERNAL PERSPECTIVE

▼ ▼ ▼ ▼ ▼ ▼ ▼ ▼ ▼ ▼ ▼ ▼ ▼ ▼ ▼ ▼ ▼

Applying the Text   15 minutes

From Hebrews 11 we can derive several "faith principles."

▶ Growing in faith often involves risk and trust.

▶ Faith-based risk usually means leaving behind comfort zones, agendas, and life directions—even when they seem appropriate and healthy.

▶ Those who operate well in the realm of faith learn to rely more heavily on God for results.

8. Based on these principles, read the following situations and determine how a faith-driven leader might respond.

a. Susan is an effective group leader and a good friend to the members of the group. However, the group seems to have stagnated. One day, several members approach Susan and ask her to be more willing to share leadership responsibilities. They suggest that increased ownership will help them grow, and that Susan's spoonfeeding has held them back.

1) SHE SHOULD ASK QUESTIONS TO GAIN MORE SPECIFIC INFO. SO AS NOT TO GENERALIZE THE WHOLE W A SUM

2) IDENTIFY SPECIFIC EXAMPLES OF HOW THEY MIGHT FEEL USED IN THE GROUP

3) ALLOCATE RESPONSIBILITY WISELY AND with clear direction

28

b. Stan tends to be an in-your-face leader, so nobody in the group is surprised when he tells them to "just have more faith" in the face of personal struggles. One day a brave member approaches Stan and suggests he show a little more sensitivity to people who are struggling. How should Stan respond?

"THAT'S JUST NOT IN MY GIFT MIX"

- SORRY MAN -

-/ QUIT WIMPERING AND GET ON WITH IT`

JUST DO IT

9. When we grow in faith we learn to leave our comfort zones. Look over this list and identify at least two areas that are true for you. Explain why:

☐ I lose sleep when people don't like me.
☑ I have a difficult time admitting mistakes.
☐ I know I should tell people when they hurt me, but I am unable to.
☐ I am easily frustrated when things don't go my way.
☐ I am very uptight when I lead, which negatively affects the groups I lead.
☐ I fear conflict and either ignore it or run from it.
☐ I subconsciously attempt to control the way others think and feel.
☐ I have no problems at all—is that a problem?
☐ I get so busy trying to do everything right I have no time to pray.
☐ I do not feel God's presence when I lead.
☐ I rarely, if ever, say, "I'm sorry."

Assignment

Decide which of the following homework electives you will do. Make sure that your choices are reasonable and will be performed by everyone prior to the next meeting.

Elective 1: Bible Study—There are six Bible passages on the next page. As you read the passages, consider what they reveal about faith and how to develop it.

- ▶ Day 1—Matthew 6:25-34
- ▶ Day 2—Matthew 14:22-33
- ▶ Day 3—Luke 18:1-8
- ▶ Day 4—Romans 1:16-17
- ▶ Day 5—Romans 4:13-25
- ▶ Day 6—Galatians 3:1-14

Elective 2: Reflection—Continue the journal you began following the first session. To guide your exploration, go back to question 9 and mark all of the areas you struggle with. Then ask yourself these questions for each one you marked:

- ▶ Why do I struggle with this particular area?
- ▶ What conditions trigger such reactions in me?
- ▶ What does Scripture say about my struggles?
- ▶ What steps might I take to begin addressing my struggles?

Elective 3: Project—Go back to the statements in question 9 and mark all of the areas you struggle with.

- ▶ Choose one and confront it "head on" by attempting to resolve it by the next meeting. It is possible that you will not be able to resolve it in such a short time, but the key idea here is to try.

- ▶ Choose one and interview a person who knows you well. Ask the person several questions to help you understand why you have difficulty in that area. Record your answers and be prepared to report back at the next meeting.

Prayer ▼▼ ▼ ▼ ▼▼▼▼▼▼▼▼▼▼▼ ▼▼ ▼▼▼

Discuss the following prayer ground rules. Add to the list or adapt the list according to your situation.

▶ *Be conversational.* The group is not a place for impressive theological prayers. Many people need to feel comfortable praying for the first time out loud—so keep prayer relaxed and relational.

▶ *Be brief.* The first people who pray in a group setting are usually comfortable praying in public. They can end up covering all requests in a lengthy prayer. A good practice is to hold the first two "pray-ers" to two sentences each.

▶ *Be courteous.* There are several ways to practice courtesy in prayer. First, keep requests personal and/or limited to intimate family and friends. This is not the time to address distant relatives or international events, which are best left to organized prayer meetings. Second, be as brief as possible when sharing requests so others have time to share.

▶ *Be sensitive.* A small group is not the place to attempt to counsel ("fix") another person.

▶ *Be real.* Most of the prayer times in this resource encourage you to respond to the issue being studied. Since the group committed to confidentiality in session 1, you can be honest about what God needs to do in your life.

Stand in a circle. Allow each person to respond to this statement, based on question 6: "I am a stage _____ Christian." Explain. Hold hands if you are comfortable doing so. Let each person pray aloud, beginning with the leader. Consider praying by name for the leaders in your group, asking God to help each of you move to the next level of faith. If you would rather pray silently, please say "Amen" aloud to let the other people know you are finished.

▼ ▼

Reference Notes

Setting: The book of Hebrews was written to demonstrate the supremacy of Jesus Christ. Jesus is greater than all created beings (chapters 1-2), Moses and the Law (chapters 3-4), and the Aaronic priests (chapters 4-10). Because Jesus is above all, Christians will experience the blessings (a key word in Hebrews is "rest") of God only by putting their complete faith in Him. Hebrews 11 is a transition chapter from the abstract ideals of the first ten chapters to the more concrete faith applications of the last three.

Now faith: Hebrews 11:1 continues a discussion begun in 10:19: "Therefore, brothers, since we have confidence to enter the Most Holy Place by the blood of Jesus, by a new and living way opened for us through the curtain . . . let us draw near to God with a sincere heart in full assurance of faith, having our hearts sprinkled to cleanse us from a guilty conscience and having our bodies washed with pure water. Let us hold unswervingly to the hope we profess, for he who promised is faithful. . . . But we are not of those who shrink back and are destroyed, but of those who believe and are saved" (Hebrews 10:19-23,39). The writer intends to explain the kind of faith with which we can approach God, the kind that rescues and protects us from destruction.

hope: Faith is a "past-present" dynamic. We learn to trust based on the trustworthiness of the person we are relating to. Hope, on the other hand, is a "present-future" dynamic. It involves having enough faith that we look to God's future with confidence. Faith and hope are always linked in the Christian life, as we leave our past to God and entrust our future to God.

what the ancients were commended for: Literally, "gained testimony." The ancients were not given God's approval for their virtuous lives (Scripture is clear that the greatest heroes each had significant sin areas), but for their faith. See Romans 4 ("Abraham was justified by his faith").

his home in the promised land like a stranger: A powerful faith image is employed here: Abraham lives as if the promise has already been fulfilled, yet he is required to live as an alien with no rights. Faith has an already/not yet dynamic.

the city with foundations: In contrast to the transient tents that Abraham and his descendants lived in, there is an earnest faith-based expectation that God's home will be unshakable and permanent.

still living by faith when they died: Here the author switches gears for a moment to provide a faith-overview statement not just about Abraham but about all faith heroes. People of faith live in faith and continue in faith even through death. Their faith does not desert them, even should they die an unnatural death (Hebrews 11:32-40).

Additional Resources:

1. Bridges, Jerry. *Trusting God: Even When Life Hurts.* Colorado Springs, Colo.; NavPress, 1988.

2. Little, Paul. *Know Why You Believe.* Downers Grove, Ill.; InterVarsity, 1973.

Food for Thought

"Magic is when we try to get spiritual control so that God acts on our behalf; it is, in effect, trying to dictate the actions of spiritual forces. Faith, in contrast, is yielding ourselves to a higher power's control. Faith involves the relinquishing of control; magic seeks to acquire control."

Tony Campolo,
The Power Delusion,
(Wheaton, Ill.: Victor, 1983),
p. 57.

Integrity

▼▼ ▼ ▼ ▼ ▼ ▼ ▼ ▼ ▼ ▼ ▼ ▼ ▼ ▼ ▼ ▼ ▼ ▼
Overview   5 minutes

❶ *Allow several group members to share what they learned from their homework (if the group did not do homework, encourage members to recap what they learned from the last session). Then ask someone to read aloud this story and the objectives that follow.*

Sunday worship was over. Allen hoped to relax before returning to church in the evening. An unmarried youth pastor, Allen was living with several other guys in a four-bedroom home.

He fixed lunch and moved into the living room, where the television was kept. His roommates were already watching his beloved Washington Redskins play the not-so-beloved Dallas Cowboys. Setting his drink and food on a card table, he prepared to settle in for a relaxing Sunday afternoon.

The afternoon would have been relaxing if the Redskins had been playing better. But they were getting pushed around by the Cowboys. Allen alternated yelling at the Redskins, referees, and Cowboys. Without realizing it, he began to snap at the other guys in the room. Then, the ultimate injustice: the Cowboys got away with an obvious penalty. He stood up and yelled at the screen: "I hate you!"

One of his roommates quietly asked him, "How can you talk like you have been talking and consider yourself a Christian leader? Would you talk like that at church?"

Not overly happy with the interruption, Allen ignored the question and continued watching the game. Later that evening, however, he recalled his roommate's words. The Holy Spirit convicted Allen of inconsistency—that he could be super-holy at church and cynical at home. Was he merely an actor, or did his relationship with God really matter to him? Because of his friend's integrity, God began to work on another area of his life.

Many leaders do not attempt to match their public and private worlds. Others do only what they feel is necessary to meet the expectations of others. But God is concerned not just with our public demeanor or our maintaining standards others set for us. God is concerned to work His righteousness in us at all times in every possible way. In this session we will:

▶ learn about biblical integrity
▶ examine what Scripture says about a leader's integrity
▶ prepare to examine our lives for inconsistencies that God may need to work on

▼ ▼ ▼ ▼ ▼ ▼ ▼ ▼ ▼ ▼ ▼ ▼ ▼ ▼ ▼ ▼ ▼ ▼ ▼
Beginning   15 minutes

❶ *Give everyone a chance to answer questions 1 through 3. The leader should answer first each time.*

1. If you were to describe the consistency of your faith and lifestyle, which of the following best identifies you, and why?

   ❏ Jesus—holy as God is holy
   ❏ Moses—walking with God, sometimes losing it
   ❏ David—heart for God, can wander at times
   ❏ Jonah—desire to obey God, much time spent running
   ❏ Pontius Pilate—wandering, frustrated, and lost
   ❏ other:

2. Who is a person you have admired (past or present) for a consistent, faithful lifestyle?

3. Choose one of the following brief situations and describe how you would respond to the leader being depicted:

☐ Mike dislikes confrontation, so he will often top off a formal gathering in the meeting room with an informal gathering in the parking lot.

☐ Marty is an extremely outgoing and flirtatious person. He can smother those in his group with a little too much physical touch and emotional affection.

☐ Mary has a tremendous amount of Bible knowledge but comes across as insecure. In one evening she can "love" a person and then become as cold as ice to the same person.

☐ Mark is a good leader and well liked, but in unguarded moments he slips into crude language and cursing.

Worship ▼▼▼▼▼▼▼▼▼▼▼▼▼▼▼▼ 10 minutes—Optional

► Consider having someone read Psalm 24 (an "integrity" psalm).

► Then, sing several praise songs/hymns that reflect the holiness of God (there are many whose titles include "Holy"). If you are uncomfortable singing, perhaps several individuals can read or recite a praise song or hymn, or the group can reflect together on the meaning of God's holiness.

► After singing or sharing, allow time to give God praise and thanksgiving for His holiness.

The Text ▼▼▼▼▼▼▼▼▼▼▼▼▼▼▼▼ 5 minutes

The word "integrity" is from the same family of words that includes "integrated." To integrate means to "form or blend into a whole." A person of integrity is one in whom the Spirit has blended beliefs and behavior in order to produce consistency. In First Timothy 4, to which Eugene Peterson gives the heading, "Teach With Your Life" in *THE MESSAGE,* Paul challenges young pastor Timothy to be an "integrated" leader.

❶ *Have someone read the text aloud. You may also read some or all of the reference notes on pages 42-43.*

You've been raised on the Message of the faith and **have followed sound teaching.** Now pass on this counsel to the Christians there, and you'll be a good servant of Jesus. Stay clear of silly stories that get dressed up as religion. **Exercise daily in God**—no spiritual flabbiness, please! Workouts in the gymnasium are useful, but a disciplined life in God is far more so, making you fit both today and forever. You can count on this. Take it to heart. This is why we've thrown ourselves into this venture so totally. **We're banking on the living God, Savior of all** men and women, especially believers.

Get the word out. Teach all these things. And don't let anyone put you down because you're young.** Teach believers with your life: by word, by demeanor, by love, by faith, by integrity. Stay at your post reading Scripture, giving counsel, teaching. And that special gift of ministry you were given when the leaders of the church laid hands on you and prayed—keep that dusted off and in use.

Cultivate these things. Immerse yourself in them. The people will all see you mature right before their eyes! **Keep a firm grasp on both your character and your teaching.** Don't be diverted. Just keep at it. Both you and those who hear you will experience salvation.

(1 Timothy 4:6-16, MSG)

▼▼▼▼▼▼▼▼ ▼ ▼ ▼ ▼ ▼ ▼ ▼ ▼ ▼▼▼ ▼
Understanding the Text   15 minutes

4. In the first paragraph the word "disciplined" is used. How might discipline help leaders live integrated lives?

5. What does it mean to teach believers with your life?

6. a. Most of the sentences in these verses begin with active verbs. Locate and circle them.

   b. What are some of the actions an integrated leader must take?

   c. These actions aren't just done by rote; they flow from deeply held values. What values do you think underlie the actions Paul names?

   d. What does an emphasis on "action" demonstrate about the integrity-building process?

7. Second Church of Antioch wants to train leaders to have integrity. Based on this passage, which of the following methods is most effective, and why?

   ❐ Require all leaders to sign a commitment to tithe, maintain sexual purity, read the Bible daily, etc. If they fall short in any one area, they are removed from leadership.

   ❐ Provide no standards of leadership other than simple encouragement to be the best person you can be in Christ.

   ❐ Form leadership support groups which practice together basic disciplines of the Christian life.

   ❐ Require leaders to spend five years in classroom training.

▼ ▼ ▼ ▼ ▼ ▼ ▼ ▼ ▼ ▼ ▼ ▼ ▼ ▼ ▼ ▼ ▼ ▼
Applying the Text   20 minutes

The members of the ministry team that Tony leads have talked about him behind his back. He has always tried to be "up front" and honest, yet his wife has learned that members have picked up on a few of his weaknesses and compared notes. The group is now unhappy with Tony, and Tony is hurt by their gossip.

8. For the above scenario,

    ❏ create an ending based on how an inconsistent leader would act.
    ❏ create an ending based on how a leader with integrity would act.

    ❶ *Allow each member to address the next question.*

9. Paul commands Timothy to be an example in speech, life, love, faith, and purity. Choose at least one of the following and discuss an inconsistency that exists in your life, one that needs to be integrated into healthy Christian living:

    ❏ your speech
    ❏ your lifestyle
    ❏ your ability to love
    ❏ your faith
    ❏ your purity

▼ ▼ ▼ ▼ ▼ ▼ ▼ ▼ ▼ ▼ ▼ ▼ ▼ ▼ ▼ ▼ ▼ ▼
Assignment   10 minutes

Decide which of the following homework electives you will do. Make sure that your choices are reasonable and will be performed by everyone prior to the next meeting.

    Elective 1: Bible Study—There are six Bible passages on the next page. As you read them, consider what they teach about the consequences of acting with or without integrity.

- ▶ Day 1—Judges 2:6-23
- ▶ Day 2—Job 2:1-10
- ▶ Day 3—Psalm 25
- ▶ Day 4—Proverbs 20:5-11
- ▶ Day 5—Malachi 2:1-9
- ▶ Day 6—Luke 16:1-15

Elective 2: Reflection—Continue working in your journal. To focus your reflections, go back to question 9 and write down the five categories listed. Then answer these questions:

- ▶ What parts of this area of my life are under God's control?
- ▶ What parts of this area of my life are not yet integrated into a healthy Christian lifestyle?
- ▶ What steps might I take to begin living with more integrity in these areas?

Elective 3: Project—Do any or all of these three things:

- ▶ Keep a "notebook on yourself" for one week in which you record inconsistencies in your life as they occur (for example, when you lose your temper at work).

- ▶ Have your spouse or a close friend keep a notebook on you for one week to note your inconsistencies. This needs to be a fun, not vindictive, activity!

- ▶ Watch a television show or movie, and observe everything in it that is inconsistent with Christian values and lifestyle.

▼ ▼ ▼ ▼ ▼ ▼ ▼ ▼ ▼ ▼ ▼ ▼ ▼ ▼ ▼ ▼ ▼ ▼
Prayer   10 minutes

Integrity is a gift from God that we must pursue with all our heart (Ephesians 2:8-9). It is not something we can create in ourselves. Allow each person to complete these statements:

- ❏ I would currently describe my integrity level as . . .
- ❏ I'd like God to help me develop integrity in the area of . . .

Stand in a circle. Hold hands if you are comfortable doing so. Let each person pray aloud, beginning with the leader. Pray for each other by name based on the statements that have been made. If you would rather pray silently, please say "Amen" aloud to let the other people know you are finished.

Reference Notes

Setting: See Reference Notes for session 1. Paul was apparently concerned that Timothy would become passive and reactionary, two responses to consistent attack. Instead, Paul calls Timothy to active Christianity and a positive lifestyle.

have followed sound teaching: Timothy had been raised in Judaism, but had converted to Christianity with his mother and grandmother. Thus he could say he had been raised (literally "nurtured") in the Christian faith. The Greek phrase for "sound teaching" is "the words of faith." Having embraced Christian truth, Timothy had been faithful in living it out.

Exercise daily in God: The Greek word for "train" is *gymnaze,* from which we get our word "gymnasium." Many leaders wrongly get the idea that they are to train for leadership in a classroom—Paul would admonish them to "get out and practice!" It is through the practice of godliness and leadership that muscle and stamina are born.

We're banking on the living God, Savior of all: Few people will work out in a gymnasium for nothing. They have an end clearly in mind. Our end in Christian leadership, on which we are putting our whole focus, is that God who continually saves us is in the act of saving others through us. We are called to believe even more.

Get the word out. Teach all these things. And don't let anyone put you down because you're so young: Timothy was to be almost forceful in applying the grace and the love of God.

Keep a firm grasp on both your character and your teaching: This phrase makes a strong connection between a leader's inner and outer life. One kind of leader can have the strongest doctrine in the world, but be weak in living out the Christian life. Another kind of leader can have a strong Christian life but not be firmly grounded.

▼
Additional Resources

1. Engstrom, Ted. *Integrity.* Waco, Tex.: Word, 1987.
2. Hybels, Bill. *Who You Are When No One's Looking.* Downers Grove, Ill.: InterVarsity, 1987.
3. Jacobsen, Wayne. *A Passion For God's Presence.* Eugene, Oreg.: Harvest House, 1991.
4. Law, William. *A Serious Call to a Devout and Holy Life.* Wilton, Conn.: Morehouse-Barlow, 1982.
5. Merton, Thomas. *Life and Holiness.* New York: Image, 1963.
6. Swindoll, Charles. *The Quest for Character.* Portland, Oreg.: Multnomah, 1987.
7. Tozer, A. W. *The Knowledge of the Holy.* New York: Harper & Row, 1983.
8. Borthwick, Paul. *Leading the Way.* Colorado Springs, Colo.: NavPress, 1989.

▼
Food for Thought

"The major reason believers don't hunger for holiness today is because they misunderstand the process that brings it to them. . . . Attempting to gain righteousness through human achievement can yield only two results, both negative. First, the strong of will can produce an external righteousness, but it is only skin deep. . . . Second, and most common, is the frustration which many people feel when that method keeps failing. . . . Without a proper understanding of how we participate in God's righteousness we are prevented from fully tasting God's goodness."

Wayne Jacobsen,
A Passion For God's Presence,
(Eugene, Oreg.: Harvest House, 1991),
p. 157.

Humble Service

▼▼▼ ▼ ▼ ▼ ▼ ▼ ▼ ▼ ▼ ▼ ▼ ▼ ▼ ▼▼ ▼▼
Overview
10 minutes

❶ *Allow several group members to share what they learned from their homework (if the group did not do homework, encourage members to recap what they learned from the last session). Then ask someone to read aloud this story and the objectives that follow.*

When I was a teen, I possessed two life goals: to get rich and to be famous. I wasn't sure if to accomplish these goals I would need to be a professional athlete (football was my preference) or to create a product that everybody needed (a difficult prospect since donuts and ice cream had already been patented).

God's call to ministry quickly reoriented all my get-rich schemes. My first two ministry positions came complete with bottom-end pay and no health insurance.

So I had to concentrate on getting famous—or at least well known. Unfortunately, my desires put me head-on with other ministry peers. In order to be famous, I would have to be the best. This meant a combination of both building the largest ministry around and rooting against other ministries.

Of course, I write this tongue-in-cheek, but it's difficult to make earthly desires appear beautiful. In truth, I was in ministry about 70% for me and 30% for God. Not good proportions.

Through a series of life-changing and difficult circumstances that continue today, God is making me face my pride and self-centeredness. I believe that I have only begun. Of course, I'll let you know when God is finished with me!

Humility is one of those words that is easier to say than it is to model. We cannot talk about making ourselves humble. It is impossible! Only God can humble us. Nor can we talk about being humble—such a statement demonstrates our pride. But we can discuss the attitudes and disciplines of life that allow us to work in harmony with God as He teaches us humility. We can choose whether to live as servants or masters of others, whether to treat their needs as equal to or less than ours in importance.

In this session we will:

▶ examine what Scripture says about a leader's humility and servanthood.
▶ discuss the tools of humility: introspection, confession, and listening.
▶ prepare to examine our lives for areas of pride and self-reliance.

▼ ▼ ▼ ▼ ▼ ▼ ▼ ▼ ▼ ▼ ▼ ▼ ▼ ▼ ▼ ▼ ▼ ▼ ▼
Beginning   20 minutes

Imagine that you are the elders, the ruling body of your church. You have just called a congregational meeting to address concerns and questions running rampant through your church regarding a recently undertaken building project. The concerns of the congregation are several:

▶ Why the Christian education people weren't consulted on the educational wing.
▶ Why you scaled back the plans without notifying the congregation.
▶ Why more of the decision-making meetings have not been open to average members.
▶ Why you awarded the building contract to someone whose bid was not lowest.

The church has a history of division, and has had its current pastor only two years. You (the elders) have done the best job possible, and have attempted to make the right decisions.

❶ *Allow everyone to answer two of the following questions.*

1. How do you feel in situations involving confrontation?

2. Describe a similar situation you have been involved in.

3. In order to heal already wounded relationships, how should you run this congregational meeting?

4. What kinds of things might the elders need to apologize for?

5. How might you cultivate an environment in which repentance and forgiveness can occur?

Worship
10 minutes—Optional

Confession springs from a humble heart and has two components: First, we enumerate those things we have done to harm our relationships with God and others; and second, we accept God's healing, forgiving touch in our lives.

▶ Consider beginning with a song of confession or penitence ("Humble Thyself in the Sight of the Lord") and a time for individuals to silently confess their sins before God.

▶ Have somebody read Psalm 103:1-18 slowly and reflectively. Each person may listen for at least one benefit they receive from God.

▶ Have a brief time of prayer so that individuals can thank and praise God for His healing, forgiving work in their lives, specifically naming the benefits they gleaned from Psalm 103.

The Text
5 minutes

If we think carefully about Christ's humanity, we realize how unbelievable it is. Why would God leave all of His benefits to become not just a man, but a lowly man? The question becomes even more profound when we consider how ornery people can be. Churches like the one in our example are a dime a dozen. Christians can be fractious and rebellious. Leaders can be prideful and self-centered. Yet Jesus came and humbled Himself, serving rather than commanding. He stands as an example for all who would follow Him.

Here Paul challenges us to be like Christ.

❶ *Have someone read the text aloud. You may also read some or all of the reference notes on pages 53-54.*

If you've gotten anything at all out of following Christ, if his love has made any difference in your life, if being in a community of the Spirit means anything to you, if you have a heart, if you care— then do me a favor: **Agree with each other,** love each other, be deep-spirited friends. **Don't push your way to the front;** don't sweet-talk your way to the top. Put yourself aside, and help others get ahead. Don't be obsessed with getting your own advantage. Forget yourselves long enough to lend a helping hand.

Think of yourselves the way Christ Jesus thought of himself. **He had equal status with God** but didn't think so much of himself that he had to cling to the advantages of that status no matter what. Not at all. When the time came, he set aside the privileges of deity and took on the status of a slave, became *human!* Having become human, he stayed human. It was an incredibly humbling process. He didn't claim special privileges. Instead, he lived a self-less, obedient life and then died a selfless, obedient death—and the worst kind of death at that: a crucifixion.

Because of that obedience, God lifted him high and honored him far above anyone or anything, ever, so that all created beings in heaven and on earth—even those long ago dead and buried— will bow in worship before this Jesus Christ, and call out in praise that he is the Master of all, to the glorious honor of God the Father.

(Philippians 2:1-11, MSG)

▼ ▼ ▼ ▼ ▼ ▼ ▼ ▼ ▼ ▼ ▼ ▼ ▼ ▼ ▼ ▼ ▼ ▼ ▼

Understanding the Text   15 minutes

6. The first few sentences of the passage contain five "if" statements. Locate the statements. How are these state-ments the foundation for the actions required by humility?

7. Based on what Paul says in the first paragraph, what were some of the problems in the Philippian church that made this passage necessary?

8. Humility is the ability to reflect a spirit of deference, submission, and focus on the other person rather than on oneself. Discuss how each of the following phrases from this passage is an aspect of humility:
   - ❏ Agree with each other
   - ❏ Love each other
   - ❏ Don't push your way to the front
   - ❏ Don't sweet-talk your way to the top
   - ❏ Help others get ahead
   - ❏ Don't be obsessed with getting your own advantage
   - ❏ Forget yourselves long enough to lend a helping hand

9. This passage mentions Christ's status in heaven. What kinds of benefits must Christ have experienced because of His divinity?

10. If you had been in Christ's position, what feelings might have accompanied your decision to become human and a slave?

11. Explain the connection between Christ's humiliation and His glorification—how does one who does not seek glory make himself worthy of glory?

▼ ▼ ▼ ▼ ▼ ▼ ▼ ▼ ▼ ▼ ▼ ▼ ▼ ▼ ▼ ▼ ▼ ▼ ▼
Applying the Text   15 minutes

Talking about pride and self-centeredness is easy. Identifying pride and self-centeredness in ourselves is much more difficult. There are three tools that enable Christians to work with God in the process of becoming humble: listening; self-examination (introspection); and confession. *Listening* allows us to hear what God the Holy Spirit and others are trying to communicate. *Self-examination* allows us to process events in our lives so that we may choose an appropriate response. *Confession* allows us to cast off sin and guilt.

12. Discuss how you might apply each of these three disciplines to the following situations:

   ❐ The last time you were together, Teri was cross with you. Sensitive to her words, you were hurt. You are wondering if she was trying to tell you something. But you don't want anything to do with her.

   ❐ You're going through an incredibly hard time: You've just had a significant disagreement with your boss regarding his ethics, while at the same time your whole job is in question due to a new round of layoffs. Meanwhile, your church is discordant, your oldest child is in rebellion, your temper is rising, and you just want to give up on everything.

13. Humility requires us to serve rather than rule.

a. What does it mean to be a humble servant like Christ in practical terms? What does it look like day to day?

b. Which items in question 8 need to happen in your life so that you can better serve as Christ served?

Assignment   10 minutes

Decide which of the following homework electives you will do. Make sure that your choices are reasonable and will be performed by everyone prior to the next meeting.

Elective 1: Bible Study—Below are six Bible passages. As you read the passages, consider what they teach about pride's destructiveness and humility's strength.

- ▶ Day 1—Numbers 12
- ▶ Day 2—2 Kings 5:1-19
- ▶ Day 3—Psalm 8
- ▶ Day 4—Luke 14:1-14
- ▶ Day 5—James 4:1-10
- ▶ Day 6—1 Peter 5:1-11

Elective 2: Reflection—Continue working in your journal. Choose one or more of the following statements that are true of you:

- ▶ I do not like to be wrong.
- ▶ I am hurt when others question my abilities and work.
- ▶ I insist on going first.
- ▶ I am only happy when I am in charge.
- ▶ I am critical of others.
- ▶ I always get stuck cleaning up everyone else's messes.
- ▶ I do not like to rely on others.
- ▶ I like to do jobs by myself—it's easier than explaining.

For each statement you chose, answer these two questions:

- ▶ Why (personality, past, another reason) do I struggle with this particular area?
- ▶ What steps might I take to begin living with more humility in these areas?

Elective 3: Project—Read completely through a newspaper or magazine. Circle or make note of each reference to anything related to pride or self-centeredness.

Prayer   5 minutes

Stand in a circle. Allow each person to ask briefly for one prayer request. Hold hands if you are comfortable doing so. Let each person pray aloud, beginning with the leader. Pray for each other by name. If you would rather pray silently, please say "Amen" aloud to let the other people know you are finished.

Reference Notes

Setting: Philippi was a Roman colony, a well-to-do city with educated citizens. Few Jews lived there, so there was no synagogue. The baby Christians in Philippi had to deal with discord and false teaching, two key themes in the book of Philippians.

If you've gotten anything: The assumption is that every Christian reading this portion of the letter will respond, "I do have the benefits and blessings of following Christ." Paul not only assumes that the Christians already possess the blessings, but he also provides material for thought. Christians reading this can ask, "Do I have the blessings of which he speaks?"

Agree with each other: We can assume that Paul is not asking people to "agree" with false teaching or those who create discord—issues he addresses in other parts of this letter. Apparently he is referring to reasonable Christians. A paraphrase of this statement might be, "Ignore those who create controversy and who are teaching falsehood. Instead, stand together for the gospel of Christ with one mind."

Don't push your way to the front: In the Greek, *kenodoxian,* vain conceit. Philippians 1:17 depicts the folly of people who are involved in ministry to "toot their own horns." In contrast, Christians are to learn to put others' agendas ahead of theirs, to make others look good. The Old Testament prophet Nehemiah is an example of such an "empowering" presence.

He had equal status with God: Two statements about the pre-incarnate Christ are made. The first is that Christ was in the form (*morphe*) of God. Some scholars have taken this as a comparison to Adam, who was made in God's image—whereas human Adam wanted divinity, divine Jesus accepted humanity. The contrast is possible. But the statement about being equal with God also refers to the outward manifestation of His being God—His equal status with God. The second statement is that although existing as God, Christ did not hold onto His "Godness." He was willing in spite of everything to give up His position.

▼ ▼ ▼ ▼ ▼ ▼ ▼ ▼ ▼ ▼ ▼ ▼ ▼ ▼ ▼ ▼ ▼ ▼ ▼ ▼
Additional Resources:

1. Hurnard, Hannah. *Hinds' Feet on High Places.* Wheaton, Ill.: Tyndale, 1975.

2. Hybels, Bill. *Descending Into Greatness.* Grand Rapids, Mich.: Zondervan, 1993.

3. Peck, M. Scott. *The Road Less Travelled.* New York: Touchstone, 1978.

4. Sanders, J. Oswald. *Spiritual Leadership.* Chicago, Ill.: Moody, 1994.

Food for Thought

" **C**hristianity, in its purest form, is not bent on human self-fulfillment. Its overriding purpose is simple and to the point: God's kingdom come. Christians, then, are those who roll up their sleeves to advance God's kingdom. They give themselves away in love, so God and others might receive. They make decisions not on the basis of economic, social, or status factors, but with only one question in mind: Does this bring God's kingdom on earth closer to reality?"

Bill Hybels,
Descending Into Greatness,
(Grand Rapids, Mich.: Zondervan, 1993),
p. 204.

Self-Discipline

Overview ▼ ▼ ▼ ▼ ▼ ▼ ▼ ▼ ▼ ▼ ▼ ▼ ▼ 10 minutes

❶ *Allow several group members to share what they
learned from their homework or recap what they learned from
the last session. Then ask someone to read aloud this story and
the objectives that follow.*

In my early twenties I began reading the biographies of great
men and women of God. These people, mostly missionaries,
became larger-than-life models for me: William Carey, Amy
Carmichael, Granny Brand, John Wesley, Hudson Taylor,
Adoniram Judson, George Whitefield, and others.

I was struck by each person's singleminded approach to life
and ministry. Most were willing to sacrifice everything, including their families (not, in my estimation, a positive choice), for
the gospel. Many of them spent hours a day in prayer, meditation, and Scripture reading. Few of them took vacations.

In my own feeble attempt at greatness, I tried to imitate
them. When I was single, I could at least pretend to be like
them. Then I got married and had three children, and my time
to be with God and to serve Him diminished. At first I felt
guilty. Then, I realized that I was more effective serving God as
Jeff Arnold than as somebody else.

This realization allowed me to focus my daily disciplines in
a positive direction, not a negative. Many people struggle with
self-discipline because they feel shame about themselves, not

because they want to better themselves. We are like the person who wants to learn to high jump but is embarrassed because he wants to clear world record heights from the very beginning.

Self-discipline is a positive exercise that may be different for each person. It involves partnering with God for our spiritual growth. In this session we will:

► learn about biblical self-discipline
► reflect on the dimensions of self-discipline: mind, body, and soul
► target areas in our lives where we need self-discipline

▼▼▼▼▼▼▼▼▼▼▼▼▼▼▼▼▼▼▼▼▼
Beginning   20 minutes

❶ *Go around the room and allow each person to answer the first question before moving on to the next one. The leader should answer first each time.*

1. The topic of self-discipline tends to evoke strong feelings. Which of the following best describes how you feel about your self-discipline?

   ❏ hopeless
   ❏ fulfilled
   ❏ directionless
   ❏ frustrated
   ❏ mildly satisfied
   ❏ other

2. Examine the following list :

   ❏ eating habits
   ❏ sleep habits
   ❏ time spent with God
   ❏ time spent reflecting
   ❏ time spent with family (significant relationships)
   ❏ work habits
   ❏ time management
   ❏ money management
   ❏ sexuality

a. In which of these areas do you have some strength?

b. Identify at least one area in which you could use some work.

3. What is an accomplishment that you are proud of, one for which you had to work very hard?

Worship
10 minutes—Optional

See the worship section in the appendix for ideas.

The Text
5 minutes

There are two significant participants in godly discipline. The first participant is God. Scripture teaches us that God is involved in various ways disciplining those He loves: molding, shaping, rebuking, and affirming. The second participant is the individual Christian. Our response to God's discipline is the most significant factor in determining how our own self-discipline will progress. This passage in 1 Peter encourages Christians to respond to God's love by disciplining ourselves for His purposes.

❶ *Have someone read the text aloud. You may also read some or all of the reference notes on pages 63-64.*

Therefore, prepare your minds for action; be self-controlled; set your **hope fully on the grace to be given you** when Jesus Christ is revealed. As obedient children, do not conform to the evil desires you had when you lived in ignorance. But just as he who called you is holy, so be holy in all you do; for it is written: "Be holy, because I am holy."

(1 Peter 1:13-16)

Understanding the Text　　　　　　　　15 minutes

"Therefore" at the beginning of this passage indicates that the paragraph is linked to the one that preceded it. The preceding paragraph focuses on God's part in our salvation and growth. It discusses the blessings that are ours through Jesus, and how suffering perfects our faith and prepares us for glory.

4. Why is it important that God's work in our lives precedes this statement on self-discipline?

5. What do you think "preparing your minds for action" looks like in today's setting?

6. Christians typically don't equate self-discipline and grace.

    a. What is grace?

b. How does setting your hope on the grace that Jesus Christ will bring you provide encouragement to change?

7. Profile the attitudes and motives of a truly obedient child. How does becoming like a child help in self-discipline?

8. *Holy* means "set apart."

a. How are Christians, like God, to be set apart?

b. What is holy conduct?

▼▼▼▼▼ ▼ ▼ ▼ ▼ ▼ ▼ ▼ ▼ ▼ ▼ ▼ ▼
Applying the Text   15 minutes

9. Examine the following list of leadership habits, and identify at least one that you need to work on:
   - ❏ arrive on time
   - ❏ perform administrative tasks in a timely manner
   - ❏ prepare when you are to lead
   - ❏ stick to the schedule; end on time
   - ❏ flexibly, but in a disciplined manner, follow a group agenda
   - ❏ don't allow group discussion to follow tangents week after week
   - ❏ keep an updated group covenant so that issues are clarified
   - ❏ share leadership with those who have appropriate gifts
   - ❏ attend to details like ordering materials and making phone contacts
   - ❏ pray and reflect so that leadership is not reactionary

10. What can this group do to hold you accountable to change?

Assignment ▼▼▼▼▼▼▼▼▼▼▼▼▼▼▼▼▼▼ 10 minutes

Decide which of the following homework electives you will do. Make sure that your choices are reasonable and will be performed by everyone prior to the next meeting.

Elective 1: Bible Study—Below are six Bible passages. As you read the passages, consider what they teach about God's part and ours in the development of self-discipline.

▶ Day 1—Psalm 34
▶ Day 2—Proverbs 6:1-15
▶ Day 3—John 14:15-24
▶ Day 4—John 15:1-17
▶ Day 5—Hebrews 12:1-12
▶ Day 6—Colossians 3:1-17

Elective 2: Reflection—Continue working in your journal. To focus your reflections, go back to questions 2 and 9, and write down all of the areas of your life that need more discipline. Then answer these questions:

▶ Why is this area so difficult to bring under control?

▶ What "benefits" do I receive from not being disciplined in this area? (For example, food can bring comfort.)

▶ Undisciplined living can be a sign of "compulsion" (fear-based living). Compulsive behavior usually covers up feelings from the past that are scary or difficult. Begin to reflect on how your lack of discipline is either a reflection of your personality or a possible compulsive behavior. If it is compulsive, try to begin understanding those feelings and hurts that need to come out.

Elective 3: Project—"The Already and the Not Yet." Create two detailed calendars of your week:

▶ Write down everything you do in a week (as you do it). At the end of the week, clean up your list and put it into outline form.

▶ Create a calendar that includes the disciplines you would like to practice. Compare it to the reality, and choose an area that you can realistically work on.

Stand in a circle. Allow each person to finish this sentence: "One thing I was challenged by in this study. . . ." Hold hands if you are comfortable doing so. Let each person pray aloud, beginning with the leader. Pray for each other by name, asking God to help you become self-disciplined. If you would rather pray silently, please say "Amen" aloud to let the other people know you are finished.

▼ ▼ ▼ ▼ ▼ ▼ ▼ ▼ ▼ ▼ ▼ ▼ ▼ ▼ ▼ ▼
Reference Notes

Setting: Peter wrote his letter to Jewish followers of Christ who were scattered by persecution (1 Peter 1:1). Because they were persecuted, they were in danger of losing hope. Many of us would be tempted to write a sympathetic, compassionate letter. But not Peter. He provided an upbeat analysis of suffering in chapter 1, then spent the rest of his letter calling believers to action.

Therefore, prepare your minds for action: A vivid statement, literally "gird up the loins of your mind." Middle Eastern men wore long tunics that had to be "girded up" when they were active. Today we tend to regard the mind as something we use to think. However, Peter says it is to be used only by those who mean business and are ready to translate thought into concrete action.

be self-controlled: The Greek word *nephontes* is used primarily to refer to abstinence from wine. In this context it challenges us to leave behind lives of indulgence and excess. We are to be sober, careful, and measured in our lives.

hope fully on the grace to be given you: Hope is the assurance that something or somebody is going to "come through." Self-discipline that is rooted in biblical hope is motivated by that hope. It has a reward to look for in the future—the grace of God. This means that Christ will lavish us with love and favor when He returns. We watch over ourselves in the meantime so that we will be prepared for His coming.

▼▼▼▼▼▼▼▼▼▼▼▼▼▼▼▼▼▼
Additional Resources:

1. Elliot, Elisabeth. *Discipline: The Glad Surrender.* Old Tappan, N.J.: Revell, 1982.
2. Foster, Richard. *Celebration of Discipline.* San Francisco, Calif.: Harper & Row, 1978.

▼▼▼▼▼▼▼▼▼▼▼▼▼▼▼▼▼▼
Food for Thought

"In fact, the Disciplines are best exercised in the midst of our normal daily activities. If they are to have any trans-forming effect, the effect must be found in the ordinary junctures of human life: in our relationships with our husband or wife, brothers and sisters, friends and neighbors."

Richard Foster,
Celebration of Discipline,
(San Francisco, Calif.: Harper & Row, 1978),
p. 1.

Wisdom

Overview

➊ *Allow several group members to share what they learned from their homework or recap what they learned from the last session. Then ask someone to read aloud this story and the objectives that follow.*

Wisdom is the God-given practical ability to discern life choices, situations, and problems. Because it is God-given, it evolves as God works in the minds, hearts, and lives of Christian leaders.

To illustrate, imagine a situation involving a woman named Jeannie who participates in a small group. Jeannie has come to a small group meeting sullen and miserable.

Further, imagine a leader growing in wisdom through the years. Here is an example of how the leader might handle Jeannie's situation at various times in his or her ministry life:

▶ First year of ministry: "What's Jeannie's problem? She's going to make everyone around her miserable!"

▶ Fourth year of ministry: "What is going on with Jeannie? I hope she doesn't detract from our discussion tonight. I'll talk to her after the meeting."

▶ Seventh year of ministry: "I wonder why Jeannie is upset. She appears withdrawn and is snapping at people. She usually doesn't act this way. I wonder if someone in the group, or even I, made her mad. I'll wait until we get into our discussion time and then I will discreetly ask her a question that allows her to share how she feels."

▶ Tenth year of ministry: "I wonder why Jeannie is upset. She appears angry and is snapping at people. I wonder. . . . I have noticed that she has been slowly withdrawing, as if something is going on in her life. She has shared about some relational struggles, and her boss is giving her a difficult time at work. I will give her opportunity to share in the small group, and I will call her and try to get together with her later this week."

▶ Twentieth year of ministry? Discuss.

As I reflect on my own ministry experience, it follows the basic track just presented. In my earlier ministry my questions and answers were simple: I asked them and I answered them. As time progressed and God revealed the complexity of my own life and growth, I began to seek answers beyond myself. This shift allowed me to listen, reflect, process, and challenge my own ideas and presuppositions.

Effective leaders are wise. They understand themselves and their own drives, ambitions, gifts, and shortcomings. They understand others. They listen to God. In this session we will:

▶ learn about biblical wisdom
▶ examine a portion of Scripture that contrasts Jesus' wisdom with that of His disciples
▶ prayerfully ask for wisdom and examine our lives to determine blind spots

▼ ▼ ▼ ▼ ▼ ▼ ▼ ▼ ▼ ▼ ▼ ▼ ▼ ▼ ▼ ▼ ▼ ▼
Beginning   20 minutes

❶ *Go around the room and allow each person to answer the first question. The leader should answer first.*

1. Think back to a difficult (even horrible) group experience you had sometime in your past. It can be any kind of group: work, recovery, church, etc. What made the experience so bad?

2. Read the following meeting outline.

   Schedule:
   ▶ Coffee—10 minutes
   ▶ Bible study—2 hours
   ▶ Sharing prayer requests—5 minutes
   ▶ Singing—20 minutes
   ▶ Prayer—30 minutes

   Notes to leader:
   After meeting starts, ask Ron to pray. Get Barb to read the Scripture passage. Last week Marty cried when she talked about her marriage. Don't give her the opportunity to break down again. Jane is too quiet. Ask her a tough question and tell the group that she has to answer it.

   Bible study (Luke 9:1-17):
   ▶ Opener—
     What are demons that you have cast out?
   ▶ Dig in—
     Did the disciples trust God to provide in verses 1-9?
     In verses 10-17?
     Was there enough food for all?
     What did Jesus do?
     What did the disciples do?
     What would you do?
   ▶ Application—
     What did you learn? Why?
     What activity should our group do in December?

3. React to this group meeting outline.
   a. What is wrong with the schedule?

   b. What is wrong with the leader's notes?

   c. What is wrong with the Bible study?

4. Biblical wisdom takes into account at least three perspectives: God's, others', and ours.
   a. How do you think God would respond to this group leader?

   b. How do you think other people will respond to this group leader?

   c. How would you feel participating in such a group?

5. What can you learn about the group leader from the group meeting outline?

Worship
10 minutes—Optional

See the worship section in the appendix for ideas.

The Text
5 minutes

Mark 9 contains the "high" of Christ's transfiguration and the "low" of His second announcement to His disciples that He must die. This excerpt contrasts Christ's wisdom with the wisdom (or lack thereof!) of His disciples.

❶ *Have someone read the text aloud. You may also read some or all of the reference notes on page 74.*

They left that place and passed through Galilee. Jesus did not want anyone to know where they were, because he was teaching his disciples. He said to them, "The Son of Man is going to be betrayed into the hands of men. They will kill him, and after three days he will rise." But they did not understand what he meant and **were afraid to ask him about it.**

They came to **Capernaum.** When he was in the house, he asked them, "What were you arguing about on the road?" But they kept quiet because on the way they had argued about **who was the greatest.**

Sitting down, Jesus called the Twelve and said, "If anyone wants to be first, he must be the very last, and **the servant of all.**"

He took a little child and had him stand among them. Taking him in his arms, he said to them, "Whoever welcomes one of these **little children** in my name welcomes me; and whoever welcomes me does not welcome me but the one who sent me."

(Mark 9:30-37)

69

Understanding the Text

6. What was Jesus trying to communicate to His disciples in the first few verses?

7. Why did the disciples not understand what Jesus meant?

8. Contrast Jesus' wisdom with His disciples' wisdom: Why was He able to perceive their subtle arguing, when they could not understand His plain teaching?

9. Why do you think the disciples fought over who would be in charge if something happened to Jesus?

10. How does putting others first (being a servant) make one wise?

11. How does being like a little child make one wise about God's intentions?

Applying the Text

15 minutes

12. Return to the story in Mark, and imagine one wise disciple present in the scene.

   a. What would that person have learned from Jesus' preparation for death?

   b. If the wise disciple had been able to hear what Jesus was saying about His death, what events between Palm Sunday and Easter might have changed?

   c. How would the wise disciple have responded when the disciples argued about who was going to be in charge when Jesus died?

13. Among other things, this passage teaches us that unwise people tend to:

❒ get "bent out of shape" easily
❒ jump to conclusions
❒ become entwined in intrigue and power games
❒ not listen and miss important ideas being communicated

Are any of these four ever true of you?

14. Reversing the four qualities found in question 13, we can say that wise people tend to:

❒ be patient
❒ be reflective
❒ remove themselves from intrigue and power games
❒ listen carefully both for what is said and what is being communicated

Which of these four is hard for you? Why do you suppose that's the case?

Assignment   10 minutes

Decide which of the following homework electives you will do. Make sure your choices are reasonable and will be performed by everyone prior to the next meeting.

Elective 1: Bible Study—There are six Bible passages on the following page. As you read the passages, ask yourself what they teach about wisdom and how to get it.

- ► Day 1—Proverbs 2
- ► Day 2—Proverbs 3:1-20
- ► Day 3—Proverbs 4
- ► Day 4—Romans 11:33–12:8
- ► Day 5—1 Corinthians 1:18–2:5
- ► Day 6—James 1:1-18

Elective 2: Reflection—In your journal, re-create two or three difficult situations from your past. The situations and their surrounding events need to be clear in your mind. Then, carefully apply biblical wisdom to them:

- ► What was going on with me at the time? What were my hopes and dreams, my fears and concerns?
- ► What was going on with those around me? What were their hopes and dreams, fears and concerns?
- ► What might God have been teaching me or calling me to do in response to my circumstances?
- ► Looking back, what should I have done differently? How might my actions have affected the outcome?

Elective 3: Project—Scan the book of Proverbs (which is full of wise sayings) and find four sayings that speak to your life. Be prepared to share these with the group at its next meeting.

Prayer   5 minutes

Stand in a circle and, beginning with the leader, complete this statement for the person on your right: "One thing I have learned about you from being in this group is. . . ." Hold hands if you are comfortable doing so. Let each person pray aloud, beginning with the leader. Thank God for what you are learning, and pray together for His wisdom. If you would rather pray silently, please say "Amen" aloud to let the other people know you are finished.

Reference Notes

Setting: Jesus had just come off the Mount of Transfiguration and healed a boy with an evil spirit. His disciples had been unable to help the boy. After that event, Jesus wanted to be alone with His disciples so that He could prepare them for His death ("because he was teaching them"). It's possible that His teaching time was not profitable because the disciples had their own agendas, so He moved on with His disciples to Capernaum.

were afraid to ask him about it: In Mark 8 Jesus had informed His disciples of His impending death for the first time, and Peter had rebuked Him. With some force, Jesus had put Peter in his place. Perhaps because of that event, the disciples were scared to interact with Jesus as He talked to them this second time.

Capernaum: Where Jesus' ministry began; it was also home to Peter and Andrew.

who was the greatest: An interesting thing to fight about when you consider that Jesus was returning to Jerusalem to die. What probably happened was that the disciples had begun speculating about who would be left in charge when or if something happened to Jesus. A fight then ensued, similar to other fights among the disciples.

the servant of all: Organizations need hierarchy; organisms need servants. Jesus had a laissez-faire attitude toward rank, position and title, but an incredibly strong opinion about service. God has a way of turning all rules upside down—death becomes life and service becomes greatness.

little children: Having established what true greatness is in God's kingdom (service), Jesus goes on to establish true spirituality (how to "welcome God" into our lives). The disciples would demonstrate their worth when they took time for the least of earth, especially children.

Flexibility

Overview

❶ *Allow several group members to share what they learned from their homework (or recap what they learned from the last session). Then ask someone to read aloud this story and the objectives that follow.*

In the1980s I planned several inner-city mission projects for an organization in my denomination. We focused our work on a block-long Habitat for Humanity site in a large east-coast city.

For one of these projects we had about 55 participants. I arrived at the site a day early to purchase some of the food supplies and to make sure that everything had been set up. When I swung by the Habitat site, I was informed that the majority of the work had been shut down because of the work supervisor's ill health.

It was a scary moment for me. I did not know the city well and had no idea what other ministries might be nearby. Besides, it might take days to negotiate work and handle logistics and materials. I only had one day.

I came across the name of a woman who ran a local ministry, and in desperation I called her. Through that call I met a former street person who had started a ministry to the homeless— while she was still homeless. She was a survivor, and she knew the Lord.

I cultivated a new relationship that enriched my life and the lives of our team members. From her we learned the trials and joys of ministry to the inner city. Yet that relationship would never have happened if our original plan had worked, or if we had stuck stubbornly to our original plan, or if we had canceled the project.

Positive leaders are able to adapt to unplanned situations. They possess flexibility. In this session we will:

► share some of what we have learned from this seven-week small group experience
► examine what Scripture says about a leader's flexibility
► discuss the filters through which we process change
► experience group closure

Beginning
20 minutes

❶ *Go around the room and allow each person to answer the first question before moving on to the next one. The leader should answer first each time.*

1. Beginning with the leader and moving from individual to individual in a circle to his or her left, allow group members to finish these two sentences for each person:

    ❑ Something I have learned from you because of our involvement in this group is . . .

    ❑ Something I appreciate about you because of our involvement in this group is . . .

2. Finish this sentence: One thing I have learned from this group experience is . . .

3. Choose one of the following four situations, and share how you would respond to it:

❏ You have a flat tire on a rainy day in the middle of nowhere.

❏ Your barber or hairdresser slips and cuts a gouge out of your hair just before a special event.

❏ While you are on a date, a waitress spills tomato sauce all over your nicest clothes.

❏ On the day you are to leave for a two-week vacation, your company revokes all leaves because it is in a state of crisis.

The Text

5 minutes

Fueled by the Holy Spirit, the early church grew so quickly that things began to get out of hand. The apostles had to deal with all kinds of situations, including immorality, false teaching, and what to do with non-Jews who were joining the movement. Allowing Gentiles into the movement created many problems. The leaders had to turn to the Old Testament, the words of Christ, and the direction of the Spirit. Acts 10 marks the turning point for Jewish-Gentile relationships in the movement.

❶ *Have someone read the text aloud. You may also read some or all of the reference notes on pages 81-82.*

About noon the following day as **they** were approaching the city, Peter went up on the roof to pray. He became hungry and wanted something to eat, and while the meal was being prepared, he fell into a trance. He saw heaven opened and something like a large sheet being let down to earth by its four corners. It contained all kinds of four-footed animals, as well as reptiles of the earth and birds of the air. Then a voice told him, "Get up, Peter. Kill and eat."

"Surely not, Lord!" Peter replied. "I have never eaten anything impure or unclean."

The voice spoke to him a second time, **"Do not call anything impure that God has made clean."**

This happened three times, and immediately the sheet was taken back to heaven.

While Peter was wondering about the meaning of the vision, the men sent by Cornelius found out where Simon's house was and stopped at the gate. **They called out, asking if Simon who was known as Peter was staying there.**

While Peter was still thinking about the vision, the Spirit said to him, "Simon, three men are looking for you. So get up and go downstairs. Do not hesitate to go with them, for I have sent them."

Peter went down and said to the men, "I'm the one you're looking for. Why have you come?"

The men replied, "We have come from Cornelius the centurion. He is a righteous and God-fearing man, who is respected by all the Jewish people. A holy angel told him to have you come to his house so that he could hear what you have to say." Then Peter invited the men into the house to be his guests.

The next day Peter started out with them, and some of the brothers from Joppa went along.

(Acts 10:9-23)

▼ ▼ ▼ ▼ ▼ ▼ ▼ ▼ ▼ ▼ ▼ ▼ ▼ ▼ ▼ ▼ ▼ ▼
Understanding the Text   20 minutes

Read the text note about Cornelius (**they**) on page 82. Whenever Jews got close to pagans, they tended to adopt pagan practices. So in Peter's time, God-fearing Jews were meticulous in their avoidance of Gentiles. Although some Gentiles had been converted to Judaism, they were kept at a distance.

4. If one extreme response to Gentiles represented adopting pagan ways, another extreme represented complete removal from pagans. What was Peter's relationship to Gentiles . . .

    ❏ before these events?
    ❏ after these events?

5. Leviticus 11 specifically spelled out which animals to eat and which not to eat. Why do you think Jesus opened the conversation with Peter by offering him unclean food?

6. Peter immediately recognized that the Lord was speaking to him (verse 14). What do you think was going through his mind when he responded, "Surely not, Lord! I have never eaten anything impure or unclean"?

7. The number three was significant to Peter. First, he denied Christ three times, then was restored to Christ three times (John 21). Now he was offered Gentile food three times. As Peter reflected on what Jesus was asking of him (three times), what kinds of thoughts, questions, and feelings might have been running through his mind?

8. The five questions below allow flexible leaders to process God's will in the face of varied circumstances. Discuss how Peter would have answered these questions?

   ❏ What does Scripture say about this?
   ❏ In the absence of clear Scriptural statements, what biblical principles might apply?
   ❏ What response on my part will help to further the gospel with integrity?
   ❏ What is the Holy Spirit saying to me, both individually and as part of the community of faith?
   ❏ What do my logic and reason suggest?

Applying the Text   20 minutes

9. Processing difficult decisions and situations through filters allows a leader to consider a subject, make adjustments to his or her thoughts, and proceed with some sense of confidence. Using the same five filters as those presented in question 8, discuss the following two topics:

   ❑ Your church is very traditional and is considering contemporary worship.
   ❑ A planning group in your church wants to abandon Sunday school and replace it with small groups.

10. Discuss what is next for your group. Since this is a leadership group, most of you have ongoing ministry roles. Discuss the following options:

   ❑ Shall we continue? If so, create a covenant. (Pages 92-94 contain a sample covenant.)
   ❑ Shall we end? If so, shall we plan a party? (See the project on page 81.)
   ❑ Shall we end for now, and pick up in the future? If so, when?

Assignment   10 minutes

Individuals may decide which of the following homework electives they will do.

   Elective 1: Bible Study—On the next page are six Bible passages. As you read the passages, consider what they teach about listening to and walking with God, who often interrupts our world.

- Day 1—Genesis 32
- Day 2—Job 1:13-22
- Day 3—Daniel 1
- Day 4—Matthew 14:22-33
- Day 5—Acts 2:1-13
- Day 6—Galatians 5:16-26

Elective 2: Reflection—Continue working in your journal. Reflect on these questions:

- In what ways am I rigid in my approach to ministry?
- What do I consider my "nonnegotiable" ministry beliefs?
- Which beliefs and principles would I like to clarify in the future?

Elective 3: Project—As a group, plan an outing or a party for fun.

Prayer   5 minutes

Stand in a circle. You may consider completing this sentence in your prayer time: "Lord, as we move on to something new we thank you for. . . ."

Reference Notes

Setting: The gospel was being spread through Jerusalem, Judea, and Samaria. It had yet to penetrate the Gentile world. Paul ("Saul" in Acts 9) had recently converted to the faith. In order to prepare the Jews to preach to the Gentiles, God had to make a dramatic statement.

they: Acts 10:1-8 introduces Cornelius, a centurion (a Roman military officer roughly equivalent to a captain). He lived in Caesarea in northern Palestine. Perhaps having been influenced by Jewish faith, he was "devout and God-fearing." An angel appeared to him and simply told him where to find Simon Peter. He sent two servants and a soldier to find Peter, who was staying in Joppa, about forty miles from Jerusalem. "They" refers to the three messengers.

Do not call anything impure that God has made clean: An important saying of Christ in this connection is found in Mark 7:17-23. There, "Jesus declared all foods 'clean'."

They called out, asking if Simon who was known as Peter was staying there: The existence of an outer gate at his home suggests that Simon the Tanner was fairly well off. Also, by law the Romans could have just stomped up to the front door and knocked. But out of sensitivity, knowing that most Jews would have viewed this as a violation, they stopped at the gate. This sensitivity suggests that Cornelius' staff was familiar with Jewish faith and custom.

The next day Peter started out with them: Although Peter probably still had questions, and Jews were forbidden to enter a Gentile's home, he obeyed what he was hearing from God and he went to Cornelius' home.

How to Prepare for Your Group

Distinctives of a Leadership Group

Groups using this resource will most likely be composed of leaders. There are several possible assumptions under which leader groups may form:

► long-term leadership support groups that function like small groups

► short-term (seven-week) leadership support groups that meet for an abbreviated period of time (every week for seven weeks; once a month for seven months) for ongoing support and training

► ongoing leadership training groups (like small group "VHS" meetings) which use resources like this one for training material

► occasional short-term leadership support groups that meet for abbreviated studies (seven weeks); then re-form in the next year for another short-term experience

Definition of a Christian Small Group

A Christian small group is an intentional, face-to-face gathering of 5 to 13 people which meets on a regular basis for a particular purpose related to the members' spiritual journey. [1]

Christian: Small groups meet for a variety of purposes: conversion, support, book studies, sports interests, and so on. A Christian small group meets for the purpose of knowing and following Jesus Christ. This is the controlling commitment at the core of a Christian small group.

Small Group: A particular relational format, different from casual conversation and different from lecture. It is a guided conversation between members of a group in which everyone can participate.

Intentional: Not an accidental or ad hoc gathering of people, but one planned for a particular purpose.

Face-to-face: At the heart of the small group are the inter-personal relationships between the various group members. Face-to-face communication is distinct from a classroom setting, for example.

5 to 13: With fewer than 5 members, it is hard to sustain the intentional aspect of the dialogue, and so the small group becomes a conversation between 3 or 4 friends. (The exception is when subgroups are formed from a larger small group for certain exercises.) When you have more than 13 people, it is easy for some members to disengage from the dialogue, so the group becomes more like an interactive lecture with only a few people who participate.

Regular: This is part of the intentionality of a small group. It has an agreed upon time schedule. Once a week is the optimum schedule, but small groups can function on a bi-weekly or even monthly basis.

Particular purpose: The small group comes together to accomplish a particular task, study particular material, or relate in a particular way. The aims and goals of the small group are defined by the covenant (or ground rules) worked out among the members.

Establishing the Purpose of Your Group

Can't we just get together and have fun? Of course you can, but unless you first discuss your assumptions with each other, you will find later on that people have differing perspectives on where your group is supposed to be going and how it should get there. Everyone has in mind an unspoken agenda and goal. The first step is to talk about those assumptions openly, and if you are so inclined, to write down a common purpose statement. A purpose statement is no more than a sentence or two describing who you are as a group and why you meet. For example:

> ► The Parents of Teens Group exists to provide a venue to discuss issues related to parenting adolescents and to develop a place for mutual care, encouragement, and growth for group members and guests.

By working through this exercise of covenanting together, you will discover common goals as well as differences in expectations. Taking the time to come to common ground will help lay the foundation for community, mutual respect, and honest discussion.

Optimum Size of the Group

Group size is optimum when it matches the leader's (and apprentice leader's) ability to adequately care for the group members. There is no magic number, but it is generally accepted that the average lay leader can adequately care for around five or six people. Therefore, a leader with an apprentice can lead a group of around ten to twelve in regular attendance. Once the group gets larger than that on a regular basis, group dynamics change and the dominant personalities will tend to control the discussion and sharing times.

If you find yourself in a group that has grown large, you can still offer a comfortable place for people to share their lives and prayers if you will ask them to break down into groups of three to four (never more than five) for discussion and prayer. Check with the host or hostess for separate areas of the house where these smaller groups may go for ease of hearing and confidentiality.

Meeting Places

A group can meet anywhere a safe, warm atmosphere can be developed. Groups can work well in any venue as long as the host or hostess has put some forethought into the user friendliness of the meeting place. Generally, homes work better than other facilities because they lend themselves to a comfortable atmosphere. Church facilities often work best for support or recovery groups that deal with shame issues. They offer more of the anonymous atmosphere many people need when beginning to deal with their issues. Groups may also decide to meet in government or work places, restaurants, or other locations.

Here is a check list of issues you might want to consider in selecting a meeting place:

► Is the location easily accessible?

► Is there adequate parking?

► Are there stairs or other impediments that might deter someone attending?

► Does the host/hostess have a pet(s)?

► How does the host/hostess feel about having a group in the house every week for six to twelve months?

► Does the location have adequate space for children?

► If in an apartment/condo/townhouse, what is the noise level from adjoining homes?

► Is there adequate room for the group to break into sub-groups for discussion and prayer?

Room Setup

Room setup is a large factor in determining the friendliness of a meeting. Consider these questions:

► Can the room be set up so that everyone is facing each other?

► Is the room large enough to accommodate ten to twelve people comfortably?

► Can everyone in the room make eye contact? (It is important that everyone is face-to-face, not in the second row or in back of another participant.)

► Is the room free from distractions?

How Often, How Long

A group gels most quickly when it meets every week. Groups can meet twice a month or even monthly (although this is not suggested as it impairs caring) if they meet weekly for the first six to eight weeks to establish a foundation for the group. A group develops much more quickly (almost exponentially) when there is weekly group contact and between-meeting contact among the group members.

Your meeting will generally work best when kept between 90 minutes and two hours in length. Some types of groups work well at one hour, especially if determined by a lunch hour or other scheduling issues.

Groups should begin and end on time. You honor the group members by keeping on schedule. Do not allow a habitual latecomer to determine the starting time. Many groups work well with a soft and hard closing time. For example, if your group meets from 7:00 to 8:30, announce that the meeting is officially done at 8:30, so that those who need to leave may do so (the soft finish). The others in the group may stay to socialize if the host agrees. The meeting should then finish and all should leave at an agreed-upon time (the hard finish).

A Successful First Meeting: Pray, Play, Recruit

The first meeting often sets the pace for the group, so it is very important.

Your most important job is to pray and remind yourself that you are in partnership with God. As you are connected with Him in prayer and are refreshed by Him, you will have something significant to offer the group.

Next, relax. You probably have much higher expectations of your leadership than anyone else in the group.

Prepare. Know what you intend to do, and in a general sense, what you want to convey to the group. However, don't get caught in the trap of having a rigid agenda.

Spend some time with your host or hostess ahead of time. Find out what his or her expectations are, and share your general agenda and time schedule. Determine what the hosts are comfortable with concerning how late group members may stay, any off-limit areas of the home, and so on. If you set some house rules for the group, or ask the host to do so, you will head off possible misunderstandings and problems later on.

Recruit leaders to attend your group. If your group is based in a church, you might invite Sunday school teachers, small group leaders, church board members, worship leaders, and even church staff. On the other hand, this guide is also effective for ministry teams and gatherings of leaders who are not based in one church. Be upbeat about the possibilities offered by the group. Make a list of people to invite. Pray for those on your list, and then invite them. An answer of "I don't know" or "maybe" is not a "no." Often people need some time to think about or to digest the idea. Give them a few days or a week, and extend the invitation again.

Finally, remember that God wants you to succeed in leading this group, and He loves these people more than you do. Prepare, pray, and then go in His strength and the confidence you have in His ability to mold you into a loving group.

FACILITATING WORSHIP IN THE SMALL GROUP

The small group offers an environment where people can learn to worship God while also learning to interact with other worshipers. The key issues in leading worship in a group are: turning our thoughts and attention totally to God; being honest; and letting God know how much we love and adore Him for who He is. If people are encouraged and led (not driven) into worship, they will grow in confidence and ability. They will learn the delicate balance between focusing on God and being aware of other worshipers. These skills, which can help you maintain balance and order, can then be used in the congregational setting as well as in private worship.

To relieve pressure on your time, you could assign your apprentice or someone else the task of planning worship.

Using the Psalms for Personal and Group Worship

The Psalms are a beautiful and personal collection of the very heartbeat of King David and other psalmists. Eugene Peterson's rendering of the Psalms in *The Message* is down-to-earth and allows you to experience the emotions of the author. The Psalms stir our hearts, making us more vulnerable to God and leading us into more intimate communication with Him.

Read a section of the Psalms. Take time to meditate on that section and then on each verse. Let the tone, the emotion, the intensity, and the intimacy expressed by the author influence your thinking and touch your heart.

Try varying the way in which you read the psalm. You could have someone read one verse at a time, pausing between verses to allow the group to think about each verse silently. You could read the psalm in unison, or have each half of the group read the verses alternately.

A Cappella Singing as Worship

If no one plays an instrument, the group may sing a cappella (without instruments). There should be one person who leads, initiates, and determines the direction and duration of worship through song. In rare instances, a group may allow various individuals to initiate songs at random, with the group joining in spontaneously. The risk in this is that the group may end up singing the old favorites of the most vocal person, rather than a flow of worship led by the Spirit of God. It is very important that the leader is wise and gentle, able to discern and guide through the possible pitfalls of this approach.

Using a Guitar, Piano, Portable Keyboard, or Recording to Lead Worship in Song

The worship leader does not have to play an instrument but should be the one who selects, begins, and ends the songs. When possible, there should be a person who plays an instrument (such as guitar or keyboard) and who also sings. He or she may be accompanied by other players and singers as necessary and appropriate. The worship leader also needs to work closely with the group leader, to coordinate with the leader's plans for the group, and to adjust the length of worship (and even the mood if necessary) to complement the group agenda. In many groups where a worship leader is active, the worship leader is seen as part of the group leadership team.

When choosing songs for group worship, attention should be given to a flow in the songs. Worship is often broken into two parts: Worship songs which focus on who God is, and Praise songs which focus on what God does.

Many groups have had success when using prerecorded worship songs. There are quite a few available today that should work well in almost any setting. The important thing is to create an environment of worship and surrender to God, no matter what musical means are employed.

Using Silence and Meditation as Worship

It is important to use silence and meditation as part of your group worship. The selah or pause that is injected throughout the Psalms is a good cue for us to take a few moments and quietly reflect. Meditation (being silent and thinking about what you have just read or heard) is good for the group, and a discipline that we do not practice enough.

Reading or Quoting Favorite Scriptures

Scripture reading can be effective in directing the group's attention to God and His desire to be in communion with us. When busy people hear the Word proclaimed and are encouraged to meditate on it, their attention and focus can be directed from their circumstances to our awesome and holy God!

▼ ▼
RECRUITING AN APPRENTICE

One of the ideal uses for this guide is the training of apprentice leaders. Apprentices are the key to sustainable growth in a small group system.

Why Have an Apprentice?

God's plan is to call all men and women and ask everyone to put his or her hand to the plow: "Jesus said, 'No procrastination. No backward looks. You can't put God's kingdom off till tomorrow. Seize the day'" (Luke 9:62, MSG).

Two things in the life of a healthy small group are generally necessary and predictable. One is that the group will attract and add new members. As the members of the group begin to take ownership of the group, they will want to invite friends, fellow workers, fellow churchgoers, and family members to come and see what's happening. Consequently, the small group will grow and eventually become a large group. However, an effective group should not grow much past ten or so regular attendees. We know that an average layperson leading a group will be able to adequately care for around five people, so with a group of ten there are already people falling through the cracks of care and follow-up. Therefore, the second necessary fact of group life has already come into play, that of leadership multiplication, or what is currently termed "apprentice leader development." It is a natural part of life to grow, divide, and grow some more. Such is the case with normal, healthy small groups—they grow, divide into two groups, and the two continue to grow.

If your group is to follow this natural course, it only makes sense to plan for it and participate in the process. Planning should encompass several questions:

► Who can lead?

► How do I recruit someone?

► How soon do I recruit an apprentice?

► How do I begin developing this person into an apprentice leader?

Whom to Recruit

Apprentice-making is not a random, mechanical action, but is best worked out through prayer and wise counsel. Check with your pastor and/or small group coordinator. Get some help in selecting a person who is interested in serving and praying for other members of the group. Leadership is never lording over others or just showing up and directing a meeting. Instead, it fulfills God's plan for all His sons and daughters to be cared for and assisted along the way toward Him. The best leaders are generally the best servants. Look for the persons who enjoy serving and helping. Look for people who have:

► a searching mind

► a humble heart

► an evident gift

► a faithful spirit

Spend time with them. Fan their fire. People are already motivated by God—tap into that!

► Tell them your vision of their potential.

► Share your commitment to their development.

► Provide them with a specific assignment: "He who is faithful with little things will be faithful in big things."

► Let them pray about the opportunity.

► If they say yes, give them a job description and involve them in ministry.[2]

► If they say no, observe them for a period of time and approach them again.

When recruiting apprentice leaders, watch for "Davids"— people who at first glance are not obvious leaders. Our propensity is to look for the person who is naturally talented or a manager in business. This has always been the way leaders and followers have leaned in looking for and choosing someone to lead them. God knew this and intervened through the prophet Samuel when he was sent to single out and anoint the next king:

> But the LORD said to Samuel, "Do not consider his appearance or his height, for I have rejected him. The LORD does not look at the things man looks at. Man looks at the outward appearance, but the LORD looks at the heart." (1 Samuel 16:7)

This amazing act of divine intervention expressed God's wisdom and compassion. God knew even Samuel would tend to go to the eldest, best-looking son. But God had Samuel look at each of the sons and hear God say "not this one," until David was sent for and received the Lord's approval.

Jesus also gave us direction and guidelines to follow in selecting leaders and apprentices. He said the people were like sheep without a shepherd (Matthew 9:36) and commanded His disciples to pray for workers for the harvest. The disciples were the answer to the prayer. The call to the disciples is the call to us, and Jesus' model is instructive: He started with them as workers. They were not hired; they were developed and empowered. Only after several years were they released and deployed as leaders.

Raising up apprentice leaders will be messy and difficult. It takes time, energy, and resources, somewhat like training little children. They are interested, exuberant, and sometimes motivated. But often in attempting to do a task for the first time, they miss the mark and get discouraged. We have an awesome opportunity and responsibility to remind them that failure is always a step in the right direction, if we learn from it. No one does it all right on the first try. Don't wait until they've done it completely right to praise them. Praise any right step toward the goal.

A Sample Group Covenant

1. The reason our group exists is:

2. Our specific group goals include:

3. We meet ____ time(s) a month, and this covenant will be in

effect for ____ weeks/months. At the end of the covenant period, we will evaluate our progress and growth.

4. We will meet on _____ (day of week), from ____ until ____ (beginning and ending times).

5. Our meetings will be held at _____ (place[s]).

6. We will use _____ as a basis for study or training.

7. We will agree on one or more of the following disciplines:
   - ❑ Attendance: We will be here whenever possible.
   - ❑ Courtesy: We will come to group meetings on time.
   - ❑ Acceptance: We will affirm one another's contributions.
   - ❑ Confidentiality: What is spoken in the group remains in the group.
   - ❑ Graciousness: We will not speak about a person when he or she is not present.
   - ❑ Self-discipline: When the group agrees to homework, we will come prepared.
   - ❑ Listening: None of us will monopolize our time together, making it difficult for others to speak.
   - ❑ Ownership: We will share responsibility for the group and our goals.
   - ❑ Accountability: We give permission to the other group members to hold us accountable for the goals we set.
   - ❑ Accessibility: We permit each other to call whenever we are in need—even in the middle of the night. My phone: _____.

8. Other possible ground rules:
   - ❑ Food (who's responsible for bringing what)
   - ❑ Child care
   - ❑ Group leadership (one leader with an apprentice, or rotating leadership)
   - ❑ Growth or Multiplication (if a priority, discuss plan)

9. Additional issues to consider in creating your group covenant:
   - ❑ Open or closed: Will our group be *open* (with new members continuously recruited or dropping in), *closed* (not open after the third meeting), or a combination of *both* (open during certain times—i.e., at the

beginning of a new book or a new year)?

☐ Service and outreach: Our plan for service (to the church, our neighborhood, or our community) and for reaching out to those outside the church needs to be discussed and developed.

☐ Fun and recreation: To round out a group and keep it vibrant, it's advisable to plan fun nights and recreational outings on occasion. Many have found it useful to add a fun time every 6–8 meetings.

Signed: _____

---

1. This definition is a reworking of a classic statement by Dr. Roberta Hestenes.

2. *The Small Group Fitness Kit,* by Thom Corrigan (NavPress, 1996), gives a sample job description for an apprentice leader.

Phone List

Name / Address / Phone

Turn your group into a community.

Most study guides are designed for individual use. While packed with good material, they don't provide much help in the way of group dynamic.

That's where PILGRIMAGE study guides are different. By incorporating community-building questions and exercises into each session, PILGRIMAGE guides will help your group grow closer relationally as you grow deeper spiritually. THE PILGRIMAGE SERIES includes titles like:

Seven Tools for Building Effective Groups
by Jeff Arnold
Just as the most talented carpenter would be handicapped without the right tools, there are key skills every effective group leader must possess. This guide features the seven most important.
(ISBN: 1-57683-020-9; 7 sessions; 96 pages)

Experiencing Community
by Thom Corrigan
Whether you're forming a new group or would like to build a stronger bond of community in your existing group, this seven-week study is the perfect "body-builder."
(ISBN: 8-09109-938-7; 7 sessions; 80 pages)

What We Believe
by Jeff Arnold
Of all the doctrines and versions of Christianity in circulation today, which ones are non-negotiable? Drawn from the Apostles' Creed, *What We Believe* examines the age old core beliefs of the Faith.
(ISBN: 1-57683-071-3; 8 sessions; 80 pages)

101 Great Ideas to Create a Caring Group
by Thom Corrigan
Many believe the single highest felt need in our society is the need to belong. To know someone else cares about us. Here are 101 tried and true ideas for cultivating an atmosphere of care in any small group.
(ISBN: 1-57683-072-1; 80 pages)

These and other NavPress study guides are available at your local Christian bookstore. Or call 1-800-366-7788 to order.

NAVPRESS
BRINGING TRUTH TO LIFE